EDGAR N JACKSON

The Role of Faith in the Process of Healing

SCM PRESS LTD

334 01405 0

First published 1981
by SCM Press Ltd
58 Bloomsbury Street, London WC1

Photoset by Input Typesetting Ltd
and printed in Great Britain by
Richard Clay Ltd (The Chaucer Press)
Bungay, Suffolk

To my friend
MARGARET F. GRADY
who planted the idea for this book
and encouraged the writing of it

CONTENTS

PREFACE

Psychosomatic medicine and the research related to it in recent decades have informed us about cause and effect processes in illness. The role of the patient in the creating and curing of illness has been illuminated. In these pages we look at some of the things we have learned.

The word 'man' and the masculine pronoun are employed in the universal and generic sense and do not refer to gender.

1

Health is up to You

The focus on personal responsibility

After a long period of mechanical and impersonalized medicine we are beginning to move towards a more individualized and humanized attitude towards health.

My daughter came in one beautiful day in June when the atmosphere seemed to be filled with good spirits and all the ingredients for healthful living and asked, 'Why do so many kids get colds during exam week?' Increasingly, young or old, we are asking the questions that focus on the relationship of emotion and health, on the connection between mind and body. When we do that there is bound to be a shift in our understanding of each individual's private role in determining his own health.

For a long period of time we were willing to ignore as much as possible this personal responsibility. We made the physician the absolute authority in matters of health. Even in the authoritarian structure of the military, the physician was the only one who could say to a Major General, 'Take your pants down and bend over.' And then with impunity and no fear of court martial, a lowly captain could give the top brass a shot in (let's skip the poetry) the major muscle system of the body.

Socially, we show our values by the people we elevate to places of authority in our culture. Two hundred years ago the clergyman who lived in the manse next to the church on the village green held this power. He was the learned person who was respected because he had the answer to all matters of life

and death. The surgeon then was the town barber who just happened to have the sharp instruments. The doctor was an unschooled and slightly trained individual who practised blood-letting and purges along with large doses of sympathy and encouragement. His power was determined by the quality of his personality.

A hundred years ago things had changed. The power had moved into the hands of the rich industrialist who lived in the big house on the hill overlooking the town that he largely owned and controlled. People feared him for his power to hire and fire, to make or break the townspeople. The clergymen and physicians tacitly worked for the industrialist, who directly or indirectly provided them with their values and their place in the community.

Now in the twentieth century we have seen another major shift of power. People are concerned with their bodies as if the body were the self. Major new construction in the community is apt to be an extension on the hospital. Health care delivery systems cost many billions of pounds or dollars each year. Health insurance and Medicare provide a portion of an ever-growing budget spent on keeping our bodies in repair. Instead of the old family doctor with his large doses of tender love and care, we are served by physicians who make appointments to see us in their temples of Asclepius with sophisticated electronic equipment and diagnostic computers which pinpoint the malfunctioning parts of our physical machinery with impersonal efficiency. And though we may spend more and more, we appear to get less and less of the type of care that prevents illness and guarantees true wholeness of being.

A revolt against this mechanization seems to be slowly developing. Old and new types of healing are being explored. As we try to read the signs of the times there appear to be emerging a new attitude toward health, new concerns in the practice of medicine and a new focus on the individual as personally responsible for his state of health.

In this preview of twenty-first century medicine we see what at first seem to be incompatible sources of medical exploration.

Yet as we examine them, we find that they have important common points of focus. So let us look at some of these forms of the healing arts that may well be brought into an amalgamation that will set the course for medical practice in the years ahead. First, let us look at the impact of Oriental healing methods as they have an effect on Western medical practice.

The Oriental concept of healing

For five thousand years physicians in China have been using a little understood form of healing that is called acupuncture. Its basic philosophy is so completely foreign to Western medical concepts that there is difficulty reconciling their phenomena with our way of looking at things. At its worst, acupuncture is viewed as an organized fakery and at its best a well-tested and fruitful form of medical practice.

Under observation of Western physicians, 151 paraplegics who were considered to be hopelessly paralysed from the waist down were treated by acupuncture, and at the end of the treatment session 124 of them were able to walk unassisted. James Reston, vice-president of the *New York Times*, watched successful surgery to remove a lung with the patient alert and conversing with his doctors. Acupuncture was the only anaesthetic used. There was no post-operative discomfort due to the effect of the anaesthetic. Several thousand deaf-mutes have been treated by acupuncture. In one study 273 deaf-mutes were treated, and in less than a year 261 could hear perfectly and nearly that many, 252, were able to both speak and sing. In another school for deaf-mutes, ninety per cent of the students have benefited from acupuncture.

When two investigators, Dr Arthur W. Galston of Yale and Dr Ethan Singer of MIT, sought the scientific basis for the method of treatment, they were quite casually told that there was no scientific basis of explanation except the fact that it worked.

Aldous Huxley pointed out that mental illness was responsive to acupuncture as it has been used for 4500 years. 'Certain types

of depression and anxiety, for example . . . disappear as soon as the normal circulation of energy is restored. Results which several years on the analyst's couch could have failed to produce may be obtained . . . by two or three pricks of the needle.'[1] This implies that life energy is at the centre of the treatment process.

In order to understand how this energy works it is important to look at the Chinese philosophy of life. Their cosmology is quite different from ours. There does not need to be a Creator at work to explain man's unique qualities. Man is part of nature and all that is observed in the universe is found in man also. Within his body are positive and negative energy flows. When these become constricted they cause malfunction or disease. To restore health the flow of energy must be restored to its proper channels. In order to understand how to do this the Chinese physician studies the meridians that mark the energy flow. In an intensive six-year course the central concern of the trainees is the discovery of the precise channels through which the energy moves and the relation of the meridians to specific organ functions.

What is especially puzzling to Western medical practitioners is that the Chinese doctor does not usually use dissection in his training. It is considered disrespectful to mutilate the dead and defenceless body. Although he has a general idea of physical functioning, his knowledge is indirect and deduced, for his whole approach to healing is from quite a different reference point.

The Chinese physician is trained in heightened sensitivity. For instance, he may spend from half an hour to three hours in taking a patient's pulse, for to him it is the most important diagnostic resource. He is trained to isolate twelve different pulses and relate each of these pulses to a specific organ function. So sensitive is this process that he must first take his own pulse to be sure of its rhythms, so that he does not confuse his body pulsations with that of his patient.

When James Reston was treated for gastritis in China, acupuncture needles were inserted in his elbow and lower legs and the pain soon disappeared. This is one of the more perplex-

ing aspects of the treatment, for the needles are inserted in body parts that are far removed from the point of pain or malfunction.

To understand this apparent *non sequitur*, the Chinese doctor explains that in the embryo the three layers of development, the ectoderm, mesoderm and endoderm, are closely related, and that close relationship at the early stages of life continues through life. Certain areas of the skin are related to certain structural parts of the body as well as to certain visceral functions, so that the endoderm, or inner organs, may be treated from the ectoderm or exterior parts of the body. In Western medicine this idea is supported by the work of Sir Henry Head, a British nerve specialist who observed that pain could show up far from the organic source.[2] So 'Head's zones' were charted, and treatment by massage and heat were applied to the appropriate zone to relieve the stress. Similarly, other medical treatment systems use somewhat similar methods. The chiropractor traces nerve routes to relieve distress in organic function. The osteopath works on the nervous and glandular system primarily to restore channels of energy towards more normal activity.

The philosophical premise for Chinese traditional medicine is based on energy movement within the patient. Apparently the skilful and precise placing of the needles can be used to block the flow of energy and serve the purpose of an anaesthetic. An American physician and his wife, both of whom are anaesthesiologists, have tried acupuncture and have verified the marked reduction of pain levels. He says, 'As an American anaesthesiologist I simply cannot afford to ignore reports of remarkable progess in my speciality in the People's Republic of China.' Another American physician reports, 'I saw more of acupuncture than I know how to believe. As you stand there watching these procedures, your scientific brain says, "My God, this can't be true." But you're still standing there watching it. I'm still not sure how it works, but I have to believe that there is some margin of truth in it.'[3]

If the flow of energy can be blocked to control pain, the stimulating of the flow seems to release a healing force within the body. Some have claimed that the process was largely

psychological and related to the peculiarities of the Chinese personality. However, in France, England, Germany and Russia, extensive experimentation with therapeutic acupuncture has produced significant results, so it is clear that the effectiveness is not something bound up with the Chinese character. Rather, it seems to be another insight into the remarkable nature of man and the importance of understanding and using his inner resources for his healing. Perhaps an amalgamation of Western science and Eastern intuition could produce a new release of the latent energy of the individual to stimulate his own self-healing. Perhaps it is possible to bring about a new and significant mystical union of the person and the universe of which he is a part, to which he must respond, and within which alone he can function. When all there is within him is in accord with what is functioning around him and through him, he may find his wholeness. All healing processes are designed to achieve that ultimate end.

The humanist concept of healing

Another facet of rediscovery of the depth dimension of man comes from serious students of psychology, the study of man's behaviour and capacity for consciousness. Scientists are again daring to speak of the supernatural. Social psychologist Peter Berger entitles a book *A Rumour of Angels: The Rediscovery of the Supernatural*. Dr Montague Ullman, a psychiatrist and psychoanalyst, and Dr Stanley Krippner, a research psychologist, subtitle their new book *Scientific Experiments in the Supernatural*. In the introduction to the latter, Dr Gardner Murphy, dean of American psychologists and director of research at the Menninger Clinic, asks: 'Can parapsychology move from the world of the bizarre, absurd and occasionally demonic to the realm of verifiable and intelligible expression of latent human nature?' And he answers, 'Dream telepathy dealing with the individual's efforts to make contact with distant reality and the social nature of man's unconscious powers, is likely to be among the sparks which will be made into a science within the next century.'

Humanist psychology, the most rapidly growing segment of psychological exploration, is determined to see all there is of man, not in the reductionist terms of the behaviourist, but rather with a worshipful open-mindedness that is prepared to believe the most audacious concepts when the evidence warrants it.

Even the reductionist methods of the behaviourist can lead to the discoveries that discredit his own assumptions about man as a limited and predictable biological mechanism. Dr Neal Miller, formerly of Yale Medical School and now at the Rockefeller University in New York, is spoken of as the 'best-known experimental psychologist in the country', and long a proponent of behaviourism. A recent book on *Visceral Learning* shows that Miller's further research tends to verify what Eastern Yogis and Zen masters have long known. He now perceives that the old ways of looking at man in terms of mind/body, willed/involuntary and inner/outer may not be adequate to describe human behaviour. 'The possibility is clearly shown that man can train and control not only his mind and skeletal muscles, but the deepest visceral processes and the activities that form the basis of his continuous give and take with the rest of nature.'[4]

It is clearly possible, then, for man so to mismanage his inner being that he produces the dis-ease that is the evidence of its malfunction. Admitting this premise, it is clearly possible for the inverse to be true, that man can so discipline his avenues of perception and bring under control resources of his mind and emotion that he can not only control disease, but may be able to prevent it by right attitudes that so permeate his whole being that all there is of him becomes the positive acting out of his healthful attitude.

Western psychology for the last few decades has been so heavily weighted by clinical observation and research that we have been preoccupied by studying sick people and morbid behaviour. We have learned much from this study, to be sure, but the exploration of healthy behaviour has been neglected. Abraham H. Maslow started a new trend when he set out to study the healthiest people he could find to see what made them

tick. Abandoning the practice of studying laboratory animals and their nervous systems to learn about human behaviour, he decided to let the person speak for himself. He picked out a number of the most successful, happy, healthy and creative people he could find and sought out what they had in common. He examined their attitude towards themselves and life to see why and how they were different from the rest of us.

Maslow found that the creative or self-actualized person had developed a capacity to live beyond himself. He was not self-centred, self-conscious or selfish. Rather, he had learned to use all of the energy of life for forward motion and self-realization. He was singularly free from the defence mechanisms that are often used to protect a person against false hazards or non-existent enemies. They seemed to be open and resonant to other people and outer circumstances because they needed none of the unreasonable protections that use up much of the life energy of many of us.

Maslow found that they were able to live free of the weight of the past. They were largely free of remorse or neurotic guilt, and did not accrete their prejudices to hamper life, but seemed able to meet each new situation on its own merits. In a similar manner they appeared to be free of the future. They were not always measuring every action on the basis of the fear of consequences in the future. Rather, they could meet the present and its needs with openness and joy, with a reserve strength that was adequate for whatever consequences might come. But they were always sustained by an inner goodness that protected them from the type of action that took advantage of others, so there was little anxiety about their past activity and little fear of the future consequences of present activity.

This ability to live life free of fear or remorse released much of the psychic energy used to cope with such hazards, to be used creatively and joyfully to make the most of the present.

The significance of this for patterns of healthful living is quite obvious. As much illness is the product of anxiety, fear and apprehension as well as feelings of doubt, cowardice and guilt, the person freed from these states of mind and emotion was not

apt to suffer from the physical processes of acting out these destructive emotions. Healthy attitudes help create healthy beings.

Maslow pointed the direction towards a concept of a super-healthy person. If health is important, achieving a superhealthy state of being would be a more inviting goal. Recent decades have produced more adequate ideas of the true nature of health. Leonard Cottrell speaks of health as 'the progressive maximizing – within organic limits – of the ability of the organism to exercise all of its physiological functions and to achieve its maximum of sensory acuity, strength, energy, coordination, dexterity, endurance, recuperative power, and immunity'.[5] The Constitution of the World Health Organization defines health as a 'state of complete physical, mental and social well-being, and not merely the absence of disease or infirmity'.

Often in the past health has been thought of in negative terms as an absence of disease. The patient has been passive in his response to an authoritarian representative of a professional health delivery system. Now that attitude seems to be changing. The personal involvement in the healing process is being explored and emphasized. The humanist movement in psychology, following the lead of its pioneer spirit, Abraham Maslow, is moving beyond old medical concepts and reductionist attitudes to look at man as a creature with great potential for healthful living and a major responsibility for that state of being.

Physicians related to the humanist psychological movement have organized the Academy of Parapsychology and Medicine with the stated purpose of 'discovering the conditions under which total healing – spiritual, mental, emotional and physical – is possible'.

The psychological climate in fifty years has changed from that of studying man as an organic entity little different from a rat in his responses to life to that of a growing awe as one contemplates the psychic power of man and its potential for creating a super-healthy being.

The Indian concept of healing

Another influence on medical concepts comes from a serious study of Yoga and the skills developed by the Yogi in achieving body control through his equivalent of visceral learning.

What we will be reporting in the next few pages comes from medical sources and is written by a professor in one of our major medical schools. It reports on an ancient treatment system that uses mental disciplines to influence autonomic body responses. Basic to the system is a philosophy of nature quite different from that of Western medicine. It claims that man is a soul expressed in a body through the working of the mind. It also says that man is often unaware of his spiritual nature, turned as he is toward pre-eminent body identification. In this basic mistake, most of our human disharmonies find their origin.[6] Much illness, from this point of view, is the result of inadequate philosophy and improper attitude.

In reality, Yoga is but a slow, deep, intelligent, re-elaboration of a very old body of knowledge, transmitted from generation to generation through the teaching of enlightened masters. The core of this ancient wisdom is found in the world's oldest sacred writings and is rooted in an advanced culture that flourished three thousand years ago.

The Yogic concept is built around two systems, a somatic or bodily system that is concerned with externals, and a visceral system that is concerned with the inner environment which can be neglected only at a person's peril. These two basic systems may be harmonized and controlled by a third man who is the spiritual or ideal man. This third man is identified as pure spirit, divine image buried in the human consciousness. This may be spoken of as the presence of God in man, or the soul as Western thought conceives it.

In Yoga the mind is seen as an organ of energy. This idea is also acceptable in Western physiology, as Lord Adrian has shown in his writings. The disciplined use of the mind in Yoga thought can use the energy of the mind to direct the flow of energy in the body. This is dramatically shown in relation to

pain, where it is reduced or becomes non-existent as the mind is directed away from the manifestations of discomfort. The conscious mind can be used to direct the unconscious mind so that the energy used in awareness of pain can also be used to obliterate the sensation. Here the learning habits and disciplines of the student of Yoga call for a special type of self-mastery.

But Yoga is not just a gimmick to outwit organic discomfort. The serious disciple sees it as a way of fulfilling his own role in personal evolution towards the spiritually activated individual. The two poles of electrical energy operating in the individual may at times be in conflict with the physical and psychological manifestations showing themselves in short-circuiting of the energy. The spiritually unified person moves beyond conflict to integration and unity of being. He uses his inner energy creatively rather than destructively.

It is the assumption of the serious exponent of Yoga that he may appropriate for himself a portion of the basic energy of the universe. He views a portion of his consciousness as designed for that purpose. His super-conscious mind has the capacity to tune in to the cosmic consciousness in such a way that the energy of creation flows through him not only in the crude physical energy patterns of metabolism but in the refined forms of energy that make him one with the all.

When the Yogi has achieved that oneness he moves beyond the usual forms of life anxiety that burn up needless energy. For instance, he no longer feels anxiety about death, for his death would be an evolving from one form of relationship to the cosmos to another and more perfect type of cosmic unity. He perceives himself as a multiplicity of universes in the quest for perfect concord. Each cell with its millions of molecules and billions of energy particles is a minuscule statement of the energy of creation. Not only is he a part of it all, but he is inescapably bound up with the basic energy of creation. His choice is not whether or not he will be a functioning part of this energy field, but rather whether he will organize his whole being so that the energy will be used to cooperate with cosmic purpose

rather than oppose it. The opposition will show as illness and disease. The cooperation will show as health.[7]

Metabolism is a constant life-and-death process. The battery of life is constantly charged with the quanta of energy that come from many co-ordinator processes. The Yogi is a man involved in the most difficult of battles, a fight aimed at bringing back to consciousness and unity the divided parts of himself. The disciplined Yogi who masters his exercises becomes literally magnetized, charged with bio-electrical energy . . . which illuminates his mind, and pervades his internal organs. Even his skilfully managed breathing is an opening upon a cosmic force field that may not be accessible in any other way. So his breathing exercises become essential to his form of discipline.

Similarly, sex becomes a resource for spiritual fulfilment rather than a mere act of physical gratification. Disease is controlled by the process that limits the inflammatory over-reaction that so often accompanies physical disorders. Even neurotic appetites that are so much a part of our diet-conscious culture are brought under the control of the disciplined single-ness of purpose that marks the well-integrated individual.

The integrated person also finds his disciplines at work in personality traits. He may abandon the fears and prejudices that are defences of the closed mind. He can enjoy freedom to grow and share life without apprehension, for the open mind is singularly free from false fears and unnecessary defences.

The healthy inner being, then, is able to heighten immunity and control while the person with sick feelings projects his negative attitudes into all of his living.

The secret of the cure of these wretched negative people lies not in the body nor in the unconscious, but in the conscious-ness. Psychoanalysis cannot cure them with its approaches. Only a personal, volitional and conscious effort, following the precepts of Yoga or of any other serious school of spiritual mystical thinking, is able to start that almost miraculous ascending spiral through which mind-power vitalizes the

body and the energized body supplies extra energy to the mind for the subsequent stages of self-realization.[8]

So writes a professor of psychiatry. So the concepts of health and the perception of the scientific student of mind and body begin to find a common ground in the processes that relate visceral learning, mystical insight and body function.

The same professor goes further. He says,

I submit that Yoga is probably the most effective way to deal with various psychosomatic disabilities along the same, time-honoured, lines of treatment that contemporary medicine has just discovered and tested.

The obligation of the individual to learn and practise the disciplines that modify his body functions and states of health becomes even clearer. The person is a decisive factor in his own states of health. So another ancient health system moves beyond the function of the body mechanism itself to understand the causes of disease and the resources for the superhealthy approach to life.

The psychosomatic concept of health

A major recent contribution of Western medicine is the study of disease as a form of meaningful behaviour on the part of the body. Ever since Dr Walter Cannon wrote *The Wisdom of the Body* and Dr Flanders Dunbar wrote *Emotions and Bodily Changes* there has been a growing interest in the way mental and emotional states affect physical functions. While we will go into more detail concerning such research in subsequent chapters, it is important for us here to see some of the major insights of psychosomatic medicine as they relate to the major premises of some of the healing systems we have been exploring. In this way we may gain some perception of other ways of acquiring a self-actualized, self-realized and superhealthy state of being.

The library of research material on psychosomatics is voluminous. In Dr Dunbar's book there are 265 pages of biblio-

graphic references, and much has happened since the book was written more than a generation ago. Yet most of this material in psychosomatic research has been used to illuminate the nature of disease with insight as to its aetiology and management. There has been no comparable effort to examine the findings of this research to tell us of the true nature of health and how to sustain it. Surely there must be much material here that could bring the nature of the superhealthy person into focus.

In poetic rhapsody physicians write of the body energies that underlie all body functions.

> Every day and all day, millions of private stations are broadcasting their physical and mental symphonies. Born in your bodies, these programs send their particular wave patterns out through the shoreless sea of atoms that surround all life. . . Today these rays and atomic disturbances given off by every human body are exciting scientists in laboratories. Dr George W. Crile feels that the electrical energy behind these rays is responsible for life.[9]

Further study shows that these rays may broadcast warnings of cancer or other morbid body conditions. The psychic diagnostician who reads auras may be taking a short cut to the information the body is broadcasting. So Dr Shafica Karagula, the Turkish physician who helped develop insulin shock therapy, claims that hundreds of her medical colleagues diagnose by psychic sensitivity and verify their diagnoses by their medical training.

It is but a short step to relate these energies to the nature of personality. Two eminent psychiatrists collaborated in a paper read before the American Psychiatric Association and said, 'Our attention is constantly focused on human personality, including not only the endowments brought into the world by each individual, but the total of the entwined somatic and emotional experiences of life. Morale is the spirit of personality.' Morale is an attitude toward life that can change the chemistry of the body. 'All psychic activity is undoubtedly accompanied by some biochemical change.'[10] So all there is of a man is in

constant interplay with the psychic energies that are a significant part of his functioning.

But too much talk of emotional roots of illness seems to
threaten some physicians, because it moves them beyond the
area of their greatest competence and security in chemotherapy
and surgical intervention. So resistance develops, as Dr Spurgeon English attests when he refers to functional illness:

> To the physician this term usually means 'psychogenic',
> although he does not always admit it, even to himself. All
> kinds of twists and turns are taken to avoid the use of the
> hated term, psychogenic. Often 'neurogenic' replaces it, and
> thus the physician is permitted to hold on to the notion that
> somehow there is a physical answer to the problem.

In hypertension the body is acting out the morale problem of
the individual. As English writes,

> The whole thing may be summarized by repeating that we
> have paid too much attention to the physical studies of
> hypertension and not enough to the emotional factors which
> may hold the key to the management of the hypertensive
> patient.[11]

'The man who can make me angry holds my life in his hand.'[12]
So a physician describes the vulnerability of the person who
loses his cool. The internal climate of an individual may be
acted out so specifically that his illness is an affirmation in
organic form of the energy of his impacted emotions. For several
years I have been conducting group therapy sessions with nuns
and priests. I have become aware of the intense anger that is
sometimes directed by nuns against priests at the time when the
onset of involution verifies the major sacrifice that has been
made to the church. As one nun put it, 'We never knew how
much we were asked to give to the church until we faced
menopause and the knowledge that we could never fulfil our
special endowment as women.' Perhaps there is some coordination between that mood and the high incidence of cancer of

the breast and uterus among women who have taken religious vows.

Our day with its increased tensions may well produce inner conflicts that show in organic form. The primitive or diencephalic part of the brain may be fighting against the cortex or the more highly developed part of the brain. As Joost A. M. Meerloo, the Dutch psychoanalyst who was one of my teachers, put it:

> Civilized and technologized, man lives in a new state of emergency: the fear of fear and the dread of disease substituting for his animal alertness. The antagonism between instinct and intellect, or as expressed in anatomical terms, between diencephalic and cortical functions, throws man into a primaeval panic. As yet, he has been unable to come to biological terms with his own overgrown brain. When this internal conflict remains unchecked, it may even lead man to psychosomatic suicide: ultimate surrender to the fear that devours him.[13]

It could be that persons with a long cultural heritage of self-exploration may have something important to tell our young and mechanically-oriented form of medical practice.

If the problem of managing illness is to be adequately handled, it seems that man must find a point of personal and spiritual integration beyond the inner conflict that makes him sick. In the variety of health systems we have examined it seems clear that the inner resource of the individual, his inner correspondence with life forces beyond himself and yet within himself, hold the secret of his new approach to wholeness. His responsibility for himself becomes basic to his health. He cannot continue to surrender his health care to others who manipulate his body chemistry or his organic function with a limited awareness of his total being and the energies that are vital to his life.

When the researches in psychosomatics began, it was with a desire to understand the cause and nature of disease that motivated the researchers. It is certain that much has been

learned about the nature of illness. But as a by-product of this research, there has been a growing awareness that the external forces intruding the body may at best be temporary and superficial forms of disease management. The sources of health are in the individual, and he cannot evade his responsibility for his own being with impunity. His role in managing his illness is inescapable, and often his avoidance techniques only verify his responsibility. The energy of consciousness is a constant force at work within to create the conditions of illness or health. The theory of entropy which shows that life energy tends to run down with age may be reversed when the individual employs his psychic energy to release his inner strength through cooperation with cosmic forces that are at work in and through him. This reverse entropy, though at best partial and temporary (for we are all physically mortal), may enrich and sustain life and guarantee new concepts of wholeness of being. Then the energy of life may be used to enrich life rather than endanger it.

The environment of contemporary science

Man is obliged to think of health in a new construct. The universe in which he lives is much the same as it has always been, but the way he looks at it has changed considerably.

Man's concept of himself is his working psychology. His concept of the world about him is his cosmology. He creates his philosophy of life at the point where his own dynamic nature as an individual functions in relation to his psychology and cosmology.

It would seem at first that it would be impossible for a man to live in any other cosmology than the one around him, but this is not quite so. Henry Adams enjoyed the thirteenth century as the high point of man's creativity, and so he recast his life in a time that was hundreds of years gone. For some people today the world is viewed through Ptolemaic eyes rather than those of the cosmonauts and astronauts. Often man looks at himself as a person in the psychological forms of Plato or Aristotle, long outmoded.

It is inevitable that people who use an outworn cosmology and psychology will have a twisted view of themselves and their relationship to the universe. When we listen to most people talk, they speak of a heaven 'up there', or a star 'in the sky', as if that is the way the universe is constructed. There is even a sect in Indiana which believes the earth is flat because an ancient scripture says so, and because the leader of the sect took a trip around the world and saw that it was flat everywhere he went. While most of us are not that simple-minded, it is still true that many of us have difficulty thinking in terms of contemporary physics and psychology.

Modern physics indicates that the ultimate reality is found in energy forms that can be perceived in mathematical equations and the formulas of radiation chemistry. The structure of the things we see, feel and use is not determined by the sensory equipment we employ in everyday life, but rather by the extrasensory equipment the scientist uses to explore and measure this reality that is known in energy terms alone. The old reality viewed by Newton in space-time terms is no longer valid from the point of view of nuclear physics. Rather, it is as obsolete scientifically as the view of the universe held by the Ptolemies.

What is true of physical reality in our nuclear age is just as true psychologically. Man is no longer viewed as a creature functioning like a highly developed animal. Rather, he is seen as the possessor of a highly refined and unique form of consciousness that is found nowhere else among known phenomena. This highly endowed creature is related to all that has been a part of the past, but is also related to a cosmic force that is pulling him into the future with a capacity for development that is also unique. Part of his nature is bound to his sensory equipment that works in a space-time framework, but part of his nature is spiritually oriented and is attuned to the infinite and eternal, the beyond measurement.

This context of cosmology and psychology cannot be ignored when we think of man and his health. If he is to achieve a valid life, it must be in terms of a valid relationship to himself and his

universe. If he thinks of ultimate reality in energy forms, it is logical that he think of health in energy terms as well.

But the energy of life appears to be a rarefied form that is quite different from the crude stuff we use to fuel our furnaces and propel our cars. This energy of consciousness does not seem to fit any other energy criterion that is used by physicists. Perhaps it can best be equated with other energy-forms that are important for life but not easily discerned by the measurements we normally employ.

We live constantly under the influence of cosmic radiation. It appears to be essential for our life. Yet it was not until recent years that men were even aware of this force-field that completely surrounds us. We would have to go underground thirty feet to get beyond its influence. Too much of this cosmic radiation could be dangerous, just as too little would impair life functions. We do not need to be aware of its existence to have it serve an important purpose in our living. It is a force-field created by the break-up of molecules in interstellar space, and it is constantly at work to meet the needs of our lives. We are immersed in it and cannot escape it, and cannot live without it and do not even need to know it exists.

Similarly, there is another force-field that completely surrounds us and is essential to our healthful functioning. It is the magnetic-gravitational force-field to which our bodies have adapted over a long evolutionary period. If this force-field were markedly reduced or withdrawn, life as we know it could not be sustained. It is essential to many important life functions such as circulation of the blood and the maintaining of equilibrium. We do not have to know anything about it to share its benefits. But it does constantly have to impinge upon our lives for us to sustain life in the force-field to which we have adapted our living.

In a comparable manner, we seem to have adapted to a psychic force-field that operates in and around us to channel life-energies in healthful patterns. When something in our being becomes antagonistic to or out of proper relationship with the psychic force-field, varied influences can work upon our being.

We can become physically ill or psychologically disoriented. We do not have to know about this psychic force-field to be affected by it, any more than the tides have to be aware of the moon. But the wisdom of those who explore man's functioning have again and again come upon this subtle but all-pervading influence at work.

Some of the health systems we have been exploring show an awareness of this force-field at work upon life and employ forms of therapeutic management that seek to bring the life-force of the individual into right relationship with the force-field that exists around the individual.

Often it seems that our therapeutic methods and our psychotherapeutic concepts have operated from an inadequate and archaic view of man and his universe. It may now be an opportune time to consider the relation of health to the concept of man and the universe that contemporary science has revealed to us. In that way we may be able to move towards our goal of man's responsibility for his own physical functioning as part of his obligation to the superhealthy creature that resides within his being.

Summary

We have looked at four systems of healing and a contemporary framework within which we must view the healing process. We have tried to fit our view of health into the energy concepts that permeate so much else in the scientific awareness of our day.

In doing that we have brought into focus the inner man and his endowments. These are so personal and unique that they can be entrusted to others only with caution. In our effort to turn all health matters over to a group of professionals we may have lost some of our capacity for personal responsibility.

The researches into the nature of consciousness and the ability we have to modify and direct it, point the way towards a new form of practice of personal responsibility for all of life and for the health considerations that are an important part of this all.

The research in consciousness through refined methods of meditation and monitored forms of bio-feedback sharpen up our awareness of personal responsibility in achieving and maintaining health. The awareness of energy potential in all of life makes us increasingly aware of the energy-processes at work within us to affect our health.

Some of the old concerns of man in traditional religious practice may be seen in a new light. In the ancient past men may have done right things for wrong reasons. In the recent past we may have done wrong things for right reasons. It may be that we are now ready to consider the importance of doing right things for the right reasons.

That will direct us toward a re-examination of traditional ways of seeking inner wholeness so that we may relate them to the insights of psychosomatic research as well as other healing systems.

Basically, our concern will be to discover a philosophical concept of health and wholeness large enough to encompass all we are learning about man and his inner being as it influences his health. Too small a frame of reference often makes us ignore the phenomena that do not fit the limiting scheme. Too large and imprecise a frame of reference may fail to bring things into a tight and trustworthy working relationship. We will try to avoid the extremes in our exploration of a more adequate relationship between a philosophy of man and his consciousness and a philosophy of health and the healing arts.

2

A New Dimension in Understanding Health

The varied ways in which the healing process is employed may at first seem confusing. Yet within this confusion there are clues to a universal quality in man that is activated by the different methods. It will be our effort to isolate this quality of being that is engaged in the healing process. When we have driven that quality into a small corner, we may then see more clearly what it is that serious practitioners in different cultures have been working with in their traditional forms of practice.

Because we are more closely tied to the methods of modern scientific research, let us begin with some of the research and insight that has come from psychosomatic medicine. Here we may begin to bridge the gap between what we call a healing process and what we identify as a faith factor at work.

Faith has long been of concern to religious persons. But it is of special interest that a group of researchers in a major medical centre have set themselves to explore the relation of faith to health.

We have by common usage become familiar with the term faith healing, but we have not so easily thought of the breakdown of faith that is involved in the disorganization or disintegration that causes illness and the need for healing.

At Wainwright House, in Rye, New York, under the auspices of the Layman's Movement, a series of seminars has been conducted bringing together psychiatrists, doctors of internal medicine, surgeons, representatives of the healing arts in other

countries along with psychologists, clergymen and practitioners of spiritual therapy. Efforts are being made to understand the forces at work to restore health and wholeness through the various forms of the healing arts.

Those who have participated in these seminars have affirmed that there is a healing force medically verified but not medically explained that is at work in and through the persons of certain gifted healers. Dr Robert Laidlaw, Chief of Psychiatric Services at Roosevelt Hospital in New York, reported that this healing force is characterized by a deeply penetrating and intense form of heat. He also claimed that the type of person who possesses these gifts is invariably a spiritually dedicated and outgoing type of personality.

Also, it is reported that types and qualities of belief are a factor in the healing response. For instance, Dr Laidlaw indicated that it is easier to get positive results in psychotherapy with a person who believes in the survival of the human spirit than with a person who has no such belief.

He further pointed out that persons with the so-called healing gift are usually in possession of certain psychic capacities such as telepathy, clairvoyance and psychic diagnosis.

Such insights point to the highly developed psychic understanding that Gerald Heard believes will be the next important development in man's control over his environment.

This seems to indicate that the integration of the being is not unrelated to important religious or spiritual states of mind and emotion.

The faith factor in healing

It is at this point that the research undertaken at Johns Hopkins University Medical School under the direction of Dr Jerome Frank has importance for us. Here there has been an effort to understand what the faith factor is in the healing process. Dr Frank points out that many therapists feel there is little possibility of a cure unless the patient has faith that he will be cured.

There is good possibility that the emotional state of trust or faith in itself can sometimes rapidly produce far-reaching and permanent changes in attitude and bodily states, though the occurrence of these phenomena cannot be predicted or controlled. The major evidence for this lies in the realm of religious conversions and so-called miracle cures. . . There can be little doubt that such an experience can in rare instances activate reparative forces which are powerful enough to heal grossly damaged tissues. . . Since it is the state of hope, belief or faith which produces the beneficial effects rather than its object, one would expect to find the same phenomenons in a non-religious framework, and this is in fact the case.

Dr Frank points out that faith cures are not limited to physical ailments which might be classified as psychogenic, but that they apply to psychotherapeutic procedures as well.

The finding that all types of psychotherapy obtain roughly equal improvement rates accords with the likelihood that the patient's state of trust or faith may be more responsible for his improvement than the specific nature of the object of his trust. The importance of the component of trust is also suggested by the general observation that the general type of relationship offered by the therapist seems to play a larger part in his success than the specific technique he uses. The aspects of the therapist's personality that affect his healing power have not yet been adequately defined, but it seems reasonable to assume that they lie in the realm of his ability to inspire confidence in his patients. In this connection the findings of Whitehorn and Betz may be pertinent. They found that therapists whose relationship with their schizophrenic patients was characterized by active personal participation, which implied that the doctor had faith in the patient's ability to improve, obtained much better results than did those who failed to show this attitude. That psychotherapy produces its effects partly through faith is also suggested by the fact that sometimes these effects occur

rapidly, and that the speed of cure need bear no relation to its depth or permanence.[1]

Dr Frank divides faith into four components: expectancy, suggestion, personality structure and status. Let us look at them more closely.

Expectancy

The New Testament says that 'it was done to them as they expected'. This truth appears to be borne out in Dr Frank's experiments to test the reaction of patients to medicines. The tests were set up so that the patients were given a placebo, an inert substance with no medicinal value. The placebo was administered by a doctor who did not know whether he was administering the drug or the placebo. The patients were told that a new drug had become available that it was thought would help them. When it was applied to persons awaiting psycho-therapy, there was a significant reduction of distress. In other tests similar results were observed. A group which received cold serum was compared with a group which received injections of salt water, and it was found that those who had the cold serum had a yearly reduction of fifty-five per cent in the number of colds, while those who had the inert substance had sixty-one per cent less colds. Evidently the forcefully injected idea without the serum was more effective than the idea with the serum. In studies of common colds, migraine headaches, ulcers and common headaches, similar results were recorded.

Following surgery, a number of patients who were suffering severe wound pain reported immediate relief from injections of a placebo.

The reaction can also work in reverse. Persons who felt they would have an allergic reaction to certain drugs had the expected reaction in severe form within a few minutes after taking the placebo. In fact, the placebo may reverse the normal reaction of the drug. Wolf reports that a patient repeatedly given prostignine, which induced abdominal cramps and diar-

rhoea, subsequently had the same response to stropine, which usually inhibits gastric function.

So important is the element of expectancy that doctors are warned against thinking that a given drug may have produced the change, for it may be entirely due to the expectancy of the patient.

> Placebo effect cannot be dismissed as superficial or transient. They often involve an increased sense of well-being in the patient, and are manifested primarily by relief from the particular symptomatic distress for which the patient expects and receives treatment. Thus, the relief of any particular complaint by a given medication is not sufficient evidence for the specific effect of the medicine on this complaint unless it can be shown that the relief is not obtained as a placebo effect.

An even stronger indication by Dr Frank of the importance of what the patient expects follows:

> Wolf believes the effect of placebos on his patients 'depended for their force on the conviction of the patient that this or that effect would result'. The degree of the patient's conviction might be expected to be influenced by his previous experiences with doctors, his confidence in his physician, his suggestibility, the suggestibility-enhancing aspects of the situtation in which the therapeutic agent is being administered, and his faith in or fear of the therapeutic agent itself.[2]

Two cases reported in a study of the effect of placebos on emotional disturbances show how the expectancy of change can reach into all the details of life. A salesman complained of lethargy and fatigue and an inability to sell his product. On being administered a placebo, he immediately felt better and sold enough goods to get two thousand dollars in commissions during the first two weeks on placebo. When the treatment was discontinued, he reverted to the pre-placebo state. A woman complained of anxiety and lack of sexual satisfaction. On being administered the placebos she reported immediate relief of anxiety and increased sexual gratification. In both instances

the expectancy of results appears to have been the only factor that explained the change in condition.

Suggestion

Often the matter of expectancy is heightened by the nature and degree of the suggestion employed. In some cases the disease is treated by suggestion therapy alone.

Such has been the experience of Dr Lawrence LeShan, who has been in charge of a research project at Trafalgar Hospital in New York. Fourteen years ago he undertook the project with a degree of interested scepticism, for it involved the treatment of cases of malignancy that were considered medically inoperable. Throughout the treatment project he was to use no radiation, medication or surgery, but through intensive suggestion-therapy alone he was to try to change the attitude of the patient and thus induce a regression of the disease.

Fourteen years later, Dr LeShan is no longer sceptical. In fact, he now approaches his work as a religious mystic, for he has seen emotional and physical changes come about that were so dramatic that they may hold a key to the problem of malignancy not only for treatment but for prevention. These cases have been carefully diagnosed and medically observed throughout the treatment process. Suggestion alone appears to have been a factor involved in regression and cure of the disease.

In our culture the suggestion of disease is continually before us. Quietly yet effectively, it is forced into the lower levels of our consciousness until it takes root there and produces its fruits.

If a person is asked to list words which describe a state of well-being, he will soon find how impoverished his vocabulary is. He thinks of 'healthy', 'well', perhaps 'euphoric', and then he runs out of words that are applicable. But when he begins to think of the words that describe illness, he becomes aware of the way even the suggestive power of language works against him. There are literally thousands of words to describe diseased and morbid states of being. A medical dictionary is not necessary,

as most people have achieved a remarkable competence of their own.

Add to the suggestive power of language the persistent advertisements having to do with drugs and remedies for all kinds of conditions, and one becomes aware of the tremendous accumulation of negative suggestion that is continually bombarding him.

The administering of medicines is itself a form of suggestion which carries with it the power to heal. Dr Frank asserts that:

> In the field of medical practice, the effectiveness of all medicines, except perhaps those which directly attack pathogenic organisms or current metabolic defects, depend to some degree on the patient's expectancy that the remedy will help him. From time immemorial physicians have exploited this by administering inert pharmacological substances to complaining, demanding patients as a means of relieving their symptoms and thus placating them. . . But recently we have learned that a placebo sometimes can be a genuinely effective agent which activates the healing of diseased and damaged tissues.[3]

Patients with peptic ulcers treated by a series of injections of distilled water and a strong suggestion from the doctor showed 'excellent results lasting over one year'.

So the evidence accumulates, making it clear that ideas are powerful determinants of health, and the suggestions that are allowed to seep into the lower levels of consciousness exert their influence in life-determining patterns of behaviour.

Personality structure

One of the facts that has emerged from the Johns Hopkins studies is that the type of personality structure a person has is a significant factor in his ability to accept suggestion and respond to the kind of stimuli that use of a placebo involves.

In the experiment with cold serum mentioned earlier, one cannot help wondering what happened to the forty-five per cent

who did not respond to the serum and the thirty-nine per cent who did not respond to the placebo. The ability to respond has something to do with the nature of the personality of the individual.

To try to resolve this problem, further tests have been made in a dark room using an illuminated frame in the wall with a parallel rod that is movable by the subject at the controls. The subject is given the task of keeping the rod parallel with the floor while the illuminated frame is moved at various degrees from the parallel. It has been found that those who are responsive to suggestion are more apt to line the rod up with the moving frame on the wall than to keep it parallel with the floor. This seems to indicate that it is easier to get a response from the person who is orientated about external factors than from the person who is orientated about his own inner sense of balance.

Schmeidler and McConnell have also found that the persons who are rigid, aggressive and suspicious are less apt to score above chance on telepathic tests than those persons who are accepting, responsive and less rigid. There seems to be emerging from such studies a profile of the type of personality that responds to suggestion and is able to be expectant.

The type of personality that is responsive to placebo therapy appears to be akin to the traditionally religious person, with a capacity for faith, a mood of expectancy and hope and an ability to relate one's self to others in a strong and life-modifying relationship.

Status

The fourth factor that Dr Frank considers in this medical definition of faith has to do with status. This involves one's attitude toward one's self in relation to other persons, and may generate strong incentives toward healing.

Dr Frank points out that many group factors contribute to the conditioning of the person who responds to suggestion. The employment of herd instincts, mass hypnosis and group suggestion may all have a part to play in this type of response. He

describes these powerful forces in relation to the shrine at
Lourdes as follows:

> Certain features are common to most miracle cures. The
> patients are usually chronically ill, debilitated, and despon-
> dent. Their critical faculty has been weakened and they are
> ready to grasp at straws. The journey to the shrine is long
> and arduous (persons who live in the vicinity of the shrine are
> poor candidates for cures). After arrival there are many
> preliminaries before the patient can enter the shrine, and
> during the preparatory period the patient hears about other
> miracle cures and views the votive offerings of those already
> healed. . . Finally, all the people at and about the shrine –
> suppliants, priests and the surrounding community – believe
> that faith-cures occur, and the person who experiences one
> by this fact becomes a member of this group and gains high
> prestige in their eyes.[4]

When the status produced by the illness becomes an important part of the patient's life, then a status that is equally
compensating emotionally is important to meet the emotional
need that originally produced the disease.

Sometimes the desire to please the physician becomes a
strong incentive. In certain group therapy procedures, recognition is given publicly for noticeable improvement in physical
condition, and this incentive of improved status in the group
produces results. Healing activities carried on in a dramatic
atmosphere tend to make the subjects into actors who play the
role of the healed person. Group encouragement is certainly a
strong motivating force towards the modification or removal of
symptoms.

So from these scientists there are strong indications that
non-medical forces are at work to restore persons to wholeness.
These forces cannot be ignored. They need to be studied
carefully so that a co-operative and creative attitude towards
health can be generated. Clearly the medical profession is
exploring these forces with interest and objectivity. It is equally
important for those who are traditional interpreters of faith to

grow to the place where all truth can be at home within the structure of their religious practice.

Then faith as medical practice uses it and faith as religious practice defines it can unite in the task of freeing the minds and bodies of man from illness.

3

Psychosomatic Medicine
looks at Man

A woman called on the phone and said, 'I do not know you and I don't really know why I should be calling you, but Dr B said he would not see me again unless I came to talk to you. Can you see me?'

A few hours later the woman was sitting in my study saying, 'I don't know what to make of these young doctors. Here I go to him obviously feeling very ill and he says, "Who is the matter with you?" What can you do with a doctor like that?'

In the time between her call and her visit the doctor had told me he had examined her and could find no physical basis for her symptoms. As he put it, 'I think she needs to talk something out, and I thought you would be the one to help her do it.'

This kind of relationship is increasing, both in the parish and among doctors and chaplains on the staffs of hospitals.

There was a time when, according to Jung, his patients wanted nothing to do with a minister even though their basic need was for a religious orientation in life. His contention was that his patients felt the minister incompetent to deal with their problems; inclined towards preaching, judgmental, easily shocked and so rigid in his attitude that the patients knew in advance what he would say. Jung would probably have been the first to admit that much progress has been made in the training of the clergy in the processes of counselling. Members of the medical profession have begun to feel a kinship with the clergy in dealing with a human problem that is larger than any

one professional discipline can solve alone. In fact, in dealing with some problems, psychosomatic medicine looks towards religion for the answers.

Relating insight to behaviour

If medicine, which has regarded itself as a science, is now confronted with the basic problems of man's total nature, it must also become an art and a philosophy. Unless it probes human motivation, it cannot deal with the roots of disease.

One of the problems that has emerged in dealing with disturbances of the emotions is referred to as 'impotent insight'. It is characterized by the ability of the patient to view his own behaviour objectively, but then not to be able to do anything to change it. He feels helpless to deal with himself because the bases for his behaviour have been explained in such superficial terms that he finds no meaning or purpose to life. He sees no reason to make an effort to change himself or move towards a goal that has no basic justification.

This is the kind of problem that Victor Frankl faces in his book, *The Doctor and the Soul*. As a psychiatrist he admits that his function is confounded unless he can create a meaning for life that has enough significance to stimulate the response of the patient. To this end he speaks of a 'medical ministry', not set up to compete with the church, but rather to face the moral and spiritual aspects of life that are an inseparable part of psychotherapy.

For it is Dr Frankl's contention that breakdown in function is bound up with a breakdown in meaning. Life falls apart when it fails to accept its major responsibilities, and in facing these facts medicine is compelled to move into the realm of values.

Man as a social being must accept social responsibility or the meaning of his life suffers atrophy. 'By escape into the mass, man loses his most intrinsic quality: responsibility,' Frankl declares. 'On the other hand, when he shoulders the tasks set him by society, man gains something – in that he adds to his responsibility.'

This approach to psychotherapy courageously faces and accepts an ethical order and man's responsibility for it. 'The task of existential analysis,' Frankl continues, 'consists precisely in bringing the individual to the point where he can of his own accord discern his own proper tasks, out of the consciousness of his own responsibility, and can find the clear, no longer indeterminate, unique and singular meaning of his own life.'[1]

So psychological insight leads to a concept of man that demands answers to the important philosophical questions about life. Unless these answers are found, man will see no good reason for acting upon his insight.

Like the man who completed a long period of secularly-orientated psychotherapy and faced his pastor with the question, 'Now that I understand all about myself, where do I get the steam to go ahead?', the physician is compelled to face the shortcomings of a healing system that is not able to ask or answer the great questions about life. So Dr Frankl concludes, 'At every step the doctor in his counselling-room will be confronted with the patient's decisions in matters of belief. We cannot quietly circumvent these; we are forced again and again to take a position.'[2]

Medicine looks at the total person

No system of therapy can be much larger than its concept of the man being treated. Even science as carefully organized and classified information is limited to a fraction of human experience. Such a limitation in any branch of science is apt to restrict the imagination in observing the whole person.

If man is viewed as an intricately balanced chemical factory, the skilled use of drugs may be able to restore inner chemical balance. Preoccupation with organic chemistry may open the doors to new worlds of chemical formulae and therapeutic agents, but to restore man to proper balance permanently, science must see him as something infinitely more than a chemical factory.

Man may also be viewed as an intricate mechanical structure,

for indeed he is fearfully and wonderfully made. The functioning of the bone structure in response to muscles that are controlled from a brain centre through a magnificently organized communication system, the nerves, is a fascinating study. It is necessary to understand it in order to repair the organism when it breaks down or suffers injury. But no matter how exalted a view one may have of the functioning mechanics of the human body, it is but a fragmentary view of the true nature of a human being.

If man is studied as a complicated mass of emotional drives that employ the body and mind, this, too, provides but a limited understanding of the totality of human nature.

From within the structure of medical science itself there is emerging a new concern for viewing the totality of man, for it is realized that disease and mishaps, as a form of behaviour, cannot be understood unless man himself is understood. But science, by the very limitations it has traditionally set for itself, cannot deal with these aspects of life that are beyond experimentation within the confines and controls of a laboratory. It is obliged, therefore, to move out into the realm of metaphysics. As Max Planck has said, 'a scientist can be a scientist for only a few minutes at a time and then he becomes a metaphysician'.[3] When he gets to the place where he asks the important question 'Why?', he is faced with the problems of meaning and purpose. Here he joins forces with the philosopher and the religious thinker.

In its new approach to the total person, psychosomatic medicine is making tentative moves towards religious understanding. It may not show a concern for some of the traditional religious concepts or practices, and it may actively distrust some of the attitudes of mind that are in conflict with its own emerging idea of what is the nature of man. But it is at least setting the stage for a meeting of minds at a point where man as a spiritual being can be accepted and understood.

A psychological view of man and his health

The psychological view of man has been as fragmentary as the medical approaches which regard him as chemistry, mechanics or emotional drives. The approaches to religion as an ethical structure, a supernatural framework or an intellectual exercise leave much to be desired at the point of seeing man in his wholeness. Our purpose is not to summarize conflicting views or find a universally acceptable formula, but rather to indicate a starting point where those who seek some common ground between the fields of psychosomatic medicine and religion may meet.

Recent years have produced a large amount of understanding of the mechanics of the human body. But even more than that, they have shown how this complicated mechanism is bound up with thoughts and feelings. The study of physiology and medical research has led to a whole new science of life, psychosomatics. Here the man that we see is in an active, reciprocal relationship with the man we cannot see, the man of thoughts, ideas and feelings.

The thoughts, ideas and feelings do not have to be true to have their effect upon life. Often the false is more effective than the true. The point of reference, then, must always be larger than any demonstrable effect. The physiological functioning of man must have within it the larger genius, the evidence of a creative mind that becomes the final measure of what is thought and felt. The wonder and the mystery of life is a concern for the religious thinker, but the evidences of the wonder and the mystery that are written into the very life activity of man are also the concern of science.

In his little book on Mahatma Gandhi, Romain Rolland makes a contrast between the methods of Western medical science and the medicine of the East. In its efforts to centre thought on the body and remedies for the ailments of the body Western medical science is, he claims, essentially immoral, for it denies the power of the mind over the body. Asserting that 'disease is the result of our thoughts as much as of our acts', he

says that any science that denies this fact or makes it easy to ignore it, works to destroy that inner discipline which is the best source of health. Gandhi 'considers it a relatively simple matter to establish certain rules that will prevent disease, for all disease springs from the same origins, i.e., from neglect of the natural laws of health. The body is God's dwelling place. It must be kept pure.'[4] Such Eastern critiques of modern Western medicine are having their influence, and the whole field of psychosomatics and psychoanalysis redirects thought to the unity of being and the effect of thought and feeling upon the body's function. Much so-called physical illness then becomes but the physical symptom of loss of inner balance and maladjustment to living.

This reawakened interest in spiritual factors in health and the healing process is illustrated in the Wainwright House Seminars where psychiatrists, surgeons, internists, spiritual healers and clergymen gather twice a year to consider in the light of their differing disciplines what is involved in the total healing process.

Dr Robert Laidlaw, the chief of psychiatry at Roosevelt Hospital in New York, affirms,

To the question, 'Does a healing power exist?' I believe we can answer with an unconditional, 'Yes'. On this phenomenal level we have testimony from healers of incontrovertible integrity and from scientists who affirm that certain rare healing processes, which they have exhaustively studied, lie beyond any so-called 'scientific' or 'Natural law' explanation. To my mind this constitutes a challenge to us to enlarge our concept of the field in which the law operates. I do not believe that when this rare phenomenon of healing occurs it is the result of successfully persuading a capricious deity to set aside the order of the universe and bring such healing to pass. I believe that this type of healing is just as subject to law as are the more commonly encountered healing processes. But it is subject to laws of a higher order – spiritual laws, if you will – about which we know so very little. When a certain

complex of conditions is met, such spiritual laws become operative and healing takes place.

Speaking further of efforts to identify how these laws work, Dr Laidlaw refers to experiments conducted by Julius Weinberger of the RCA Laboratories of New York which assume that magnetism and electric fields are concomitants of this healing force.

In England the Society of Radiaesthesia is devising instruments to measure this power which is believed to be akin to radioactivity. In some preliminary experiments, Mr Weinberger has attached dental X-ray films to the hands of a healer during healing, and has found on them evidence indicating radiation of the general nature of high energy X-rays.[5]

More recent studies in the Soviet Union in what is called Kirlian photography appear to support the concept of radiation of some sort eminating from the fingers and hands of certain persons.

For decades the prevalent attitudes of the physical sciences that were essentially mechanistic exerted a strong influence on the medical sciences, with man treated essentially as a chemical or mechanical entity. As one medical school professor put it, 'Man has a soul and a body. That's enough for the soul. For the next four years I shall be talking to you about the body.' In an atmosphere of chemical and mechanical concern the soul was easily dismissed. But the soul of man never stays dismissed for long. A prominent physician speaking before the New York Academy of Medicine a few years ago said, 'There is something here above and beyond the test tube which must come back into the relationship between the patient and the physician.'

The human body is a marvellous chemical plant with many complicated processes of change and assimilation going on all the time. This body chemistry is important for health and understanding. It is important for self-knowledge. But if we think we can know all about man by understanding his body chemistry, we have a very limited idea of his nature. Important

mechanical principles are employed in the relation of muscle and bone, the pumping action of the heart and the bellows we call the lungs; but knowing all there is to know about this mechanical functioning will not open the door to the mystery of man's spiritual nature. The emphasis on energy that is central in the new physics changes the direction of our thinking about man from a chemical or mechanical being to a more precisely power-filled being. Modern medicine is increasingly aware of these unexplored and yet important frontiers of being which give clues to man's spiritual nature.

The problem of definition here becomes difficult. If man is seen as complicated chemistry, he can be defined within a chemical frame of reference. If he is a complicated machine, his nature can be defined in mechanical terms. But if man is more than these, he can be understood only with reference to this something more. The religious mind has always been aware of this something more but has never been able to define it precisely enough to satisfy the scientific mind. To say that man has a spiritual nature which is reflected in spiritual activity may be true but it is not definitive. To say that there are potential powers within the human that are psychic in nature and are not bound by the convenient measurements of space and time may be true but not definitive. Perhaps it is important to realize that as long as this quality of being is 'above and beyond the test tube', it will not be possible to give it a definition that would fit the demands of precise and scientific measurement. But this does not limit the obligation to observe and explore with the realization that frames of reference are also merely conveniences to assist the mind in its orderly approach to reality. When the nature of reality is larger than the frame of reference with which it works, the mode of thought must be modified and not the evidence of reality. That there is some power operative within man which is the evidence of an orderly and creative intelligence, and that this power is subject to a framework of laws that is spiritual in nature, is perhaps all we need to have as a working premise in evaluating our response to it.

It is perhaps significant that the studies of man's physical

and organic response to life are the source of some of the clearest insight into his non-physical nature. Psychosomatic medicine has clearly established the power of ideas over the functioning of the physical organism. Some people choose illness as a way of life. Some choose their illnesses, often unconsciously, to suit their emotional needs. Their ideas about themselves and about their relationships to other people bear fruit in their symptoms. Instead of asking 'What is the matter with you?' it may be more realistic to ask, 'Who is the matter with you?' Their illnesses are no less real because of their psychogenic nature, but the treatment of them is never complete until the ideas behind them are brought into clear focus.

Flanders Dunbar writes,

> Just as the colitic patient has his attitude focused on dying, partly out of hopelessness, partly to make those who should have loved him sorry, and partly to punish himself for his unworthiness, so his loved ones react to illness with feelings of hopelessness and guilt, even to the extent of becoming ill themselves or dying as a reaction to the death of the colitic sufferer.

In such cases deep feelings of despair reflect themselves in the physical symptoms acquired by the sufferer.

Dr Dunbar says that there are,

> two types of patient who are most discouraging from the doctor's point of view. One is the patient who makes him sick (literally, not in any idiomatic sense of the word) from emotional contagion or irritation. The other is the patient who aggravates the physician's own ailments by displaying the same symptoms or by confounding medical wisdom by refusing to get well.[6]

Here the physician marks the patient with ideas of illness so strong that medical practice is ineffective, but more than that, the patient can be so strong in his ideas that he even makes the doctor sick. This implies that ill-health, like good health, may

be communicated by the ideas that possess people and are transmitted by them.

E. Weaver Johnson reports that the diabetic is often suffering from unresolved grief.[7] The production of blood sugar to compensate the body's reaction to acute grief is so excessive that the glands are taxed to the breaking point. What they can handle on a temporary basis is too much for them on a chronic basis, and the diabetes is the result. The emotion of grief which has complicated roots in the feelings of a person may reflect itself in a complicated set of symptoms, of which diabetes may be but one. According to Erich Lindemann, ulcerative colitis may be another, and Lawrence LeShan correlates cancer with grief in certain instances.

Karl Menninger points out that the mildly self-destructive types of addiction, such as tobacco and alcohol, may also have their roots in the emotional needs of the person who would punish himself or others for real or imagined guilt.

Franz Alexander feels that, 'Chronically increased muscle tension brought about by sustained aggressive impulses appear to be a pathogenic factor in rheumatoid arthritis.' So anger constricts and cripples the physical organism. He further finds that the disease often develops with 'unconscious rebellion', of guilt at the 'death of a hated dependent relative' or at the obligation to accept the female role in life which is essentially unacceptable. In each instance the root problem deals with an idea about the self in relation to other people, and the problem involves the emotion of love or the ability creatively to express love.

While recognizing that there are physiological factors that may be conducive to asthmatic attacks, Alexander points out that these are usually stimulated by emotional states.

A great variety of emotional factors have been mentioned by different observers; they include almost any sudden intensive emotional stimulus – sexual excitation, anxiety, jealousy and rage . . . we find among persons suffering from asthma many types of personalities: aggressive, ambitious, argumentative

persons, daredevils, and also hypersensitive, aesthetic types. . . Hostile impulses directed against the love object may also threaten the dependent relationship and provoke an attack.[8]

The feelings become a major contributive cause of the acute attack.

The response of that faithful little muscle, the heart, to the stress of emotion is well known in literature and medical study. Dr Dunbar says,

> The relationship between the particular kind of cardiac trouble which the individual develops and his whole background of psychic experience has been well established. . . the heart does not exist all by itself, isolated from the rest of the body. . . In human beings the heart is inseparable from the whole individual. If the whole individual is kept well, the broken heart can be left to the poets.[9]

The effort to be top dog, severe judgments of self and others, and persistent anxiety and guilt, seem to be the major contributive factors in heart disease.

Summing up the insights of psychosomatic research, Dr Johnson concludes,

> The cause is within us. The cure is within us. When we know this, our concept of disease is no longer that of something fixed upon the body cells which must be purged, cut or burned away. It is not something coming from the outside which we cannot prevent. Rather, it is a change from within, and we must find the reason why the body changes its perfect pattern to vibrate to discord rather than to harmony. Psychosomatic research is helping us to find the clues. Incidentally, it is changing the whole attitude and approach of medicine toward the problem of sick bodies and confused minds.

Faith in preventive and restorative processes

The directing of medical interest towards the religious concern for the whole man is reflected in the Wainwright House seminars previously referred to. Here the effort is made to understand the cause-effect relationships that produce ill health as well as the healing powers within the person that can be released through religious influence. The seminars reveal the medical man as also the religious man, with a devoted concern that every agency of health be understood and developed for the use of man.

Speaking from the point of view of a person disciplined in the science of medicine, Dr Howard T. Craven, a Washington surgeon, spoke to his colleagues at the Wainwright Seminar about the relation of religious values to the healing process.

> There is no question in my mind but that without the presence of Jesus Christ in a room, healing does not take place. I know that Jesus Christ heals through people. . . I feel convinced that we are on the verge of a break-through in the field of healing. I have come to the conclusion that there are four basic, fundamental areas. The first is the medical viewpoint; if people do not have the benefit of medicine, they feel guilty. Number two, they must have the benefit of psychiatry, because if they don't, they feel guilty. After you have done those things, then you must go straight to God, if you have not had a healing in those other areas. By using this approach . . . it has been possible sometimes in only a week to change their attitude towards their situation, towards their fellow-man, towards God and towards the future so that, for all practical purposes, their physical symptoms disappear. I am convinced that there is no incurable disease; there are only incurable people, and the only reason we don't cure these people is because we don't ask God's guidance in how to find a channel to that person. When we become humble enough for that, when we can become clear enough channels for that, chronic incurable disease will vanish from the face of the earth.
>
> People get sick in two ways. The first is that which orthodox

medicine sees; you get sick because you are weak. That is what I had always believed. But looking at myself (referring to his own illness) . . . it was obvious that this was not true. . . . Therefore, I had to take a different tack. I had to grasp the idea that perhaps the reason people became sick was because they were so highly involved and so much superior to the average that they rejected this aspect of personality. Dr Howe, of England, made the statement that no one would become physically, intellectually, morally or spiritually ill unless he was trying to reject some portion of his experience.

Exploring further the implications of the rejection of his spiritual nature and the healing power that existed there, Dr Craven described an experience that illustrated the surgeon's use of this higher power.

Once I was asked to lead a prayer group for a baby who had a brain abscess. I thought of myself as a mirror, using the group as a source of creative power. I told the group what to do with a brain abscess surgically, how you make an incision, and how to drain the abscess, and put back the bone, and sew the skin cap back. We 'saw' that. Then we 'saw' Jesus touching that. And then, since I know that children usually get sick not because of what happens to them but because of what their mothers and fathers are doing wrong, we prayed the same way for the mother and father . . . we found that at that moment the baby's temperature had gone down from 104 to normal. You can't say that I knew what I was doing. . . Obviously this is something that anybody can do.

In response to Dr Craven's illustration of the employment of the healing power of prayer, Mrs Elined Kitschnig, a psychotherapist from Washington, DC, raised the question whether this power could be used destructively as well as creatively, depending upon the attitude of the person who used it.

I have done a certain amount of physical coordination work, along lines of Alexander's and Lee's techniques. Dealing with patients in that way, dealing with their physical coordination,

I feel this thing that has been described here in my hands. But I have been very chary of its usage. I feel a shyness, an awe, and legitimate fear and caution, because it seems to me that it is even stronger than psychotherapy.

To my way of thinking, physical things are, as it were, the copper, and the emotional level is the silver, and the spiritual is the gold. One can be converted into the other. But the least conscious is the physical, and in it is tied up the whole atomic energy of the psyche. If it is dealt with wrongly and lays hold of that in the therapist which is vulnerable, then the danger of what can be released is that much greater when we are dealing with the emotional realm.

And I would really like to know, from you who deal in physical healing, whether it is because you walk, like naive children, through the dangers and don't know they are there, whether at any moment at some crisis of your life you may be caught and your fall be all the worse because of your naiveté; or whether it is that you are more divinely protected than the psychotherapists. Or do we psychotherapists misunderstand the whole situation?

Individuality in the healing process

The problem of the employment of what Dr Laidlaw called 'the healing power' is inevitably bound up with the personality and the motivation of the one who employs it. Certainly this was a central concern of Jesus at the time of his temptation. Was his central power of spirit to be used for selfish purposes? Was it to be used to attract attention and appeal to the love of the spectacular? Was it to be a bargaining power for physical or temporal influence? To all of these temptations Jesus answered a resounding 'No'. With complete selflessness of purpose he was determined to work quietly and with respect for the power of faith in himself and others, so that the full impact of this realm of spiritual law and order might be revealed, even though the effect of this higher order of law stimulated such a violent

response on the part of those who were devoted to material things that he would be crucified as a result.

Dr Laidlaw describes the attitudes and motivation of those he had examined who exploited this power effectively.

> Here we have gained our greatest insight into the question by an examination of the individual healer. Many and interesting, especially to the psychiatrist, are the things we have learned about him. Here are a few. First of all he must be one who elicits rather than inhibits. He must be a 'resonant cavity', an 'instrument', an 'open channel'. He must be relaxed. His senses must be highly acute. He must be a 'dedicated person', devoted to the well-being of his patient. He must be in a state of 'open-ness', of conscious or unconscious prayer; he must have expectancy and faith. His gift often involves para-normal powers such as telepathy and clairvoyance. Perhaps one might say that though not all sensitives are healers, most healers are to some degree sensitives. Here are the beginnings of a personality profile.[10]

To this point in our consideration of the important matter of health, we have used insights only from those who work within the disciplined sciences. Yet the insights of psychosomatic medicine sound strangely familiar to those who have long had a religious orientation. The diseases of the body are not separated from the conditions of the spirit, and the nature of the spirit is beyond the easy access of scientific inquiry. The scientific insight that verifies the power of faith to heal gives to the practice of applied religion a new responsibility in the minds of those who are truly concerned about the well-being of the human personality.

The body that is explored from the point of view of the medical scientist who employs all of the best insights of physics, chemistry and psychology is a sensitive and mysterious constellation of living quality that affirms in many ways its essential spiritual nature. So the science of life and health quickly moves beyond the merely physical to those qualities of being that are produced within bodily relationships. So there may be a rela-

tionship between body and spirit not unlike the relationship between brain and mind.

The contribution of modern science in stating the nature of the body as a spiritually sensitive, faith-responding organization of life prepares the way for a working relationship between science and religion that should be as rewarding as it is demanding. Both science and religion will have to modify some of their preconceived ideas about man to make room for the clearer picture of his nature that is emerging.

Because this idea of the relation of faith to the healing process is rather unusual, we must approach it with caution. We must not be swept off our feet by partial views concerning the relation of the individual and health. When this is done, we are in danger of equally dangerous forms of injury.

In understanding the man who gets sick in contrast to understanding the illness that the man gets, it is important to see the total relationship of the man to himself and his environment.

When medicine was practised with materialistic presuppositions, it was easier to think of therapy as chemical adjustment or surgical modification. The materialistic view of man is no longer tenable. When we think of illness and health we are obliged to look at the man who becomes ill and the personal and social factors that impinge upon his life.

But the approach to man as a spiritual being is complicated. The dangers in this direction are shown by the extremist attitudes toward healing and the medical profession. To have so materialistic an understanding of health that all spiritual considerations are ruled out is comparable to having so spiritual an understanding of health that other important points of view are excluded.

Christian Science denies the reality of disease and employs powerful suggestion to create the illusion of life as non-material. Such an approach to disease destroys the capacity to make distinctions between physical conditions that differ as to origin and treatment. The spiritual view of man and his nature recognizes the power of spiritual forces at work in life without

denying the reality of the material agencies through which that force works. Any system of thought that tends to obliterate man's capacity to make distinctions, and interfere with his ability to classify experience with proper concern for origins, and fails to see the validity of proper categories for the experience of life, weakens the ultimate and valid use of spiritual insight. Spiritual insight at its best does not weaken man's reality sense, nor does it deny the validity of the destructive agents at work in life. It does try to develop and direct forces in man which can face all there is of destructive reality with resources of spirit that are strong enough to assert the creative, restorative factor in life.

The philosophical non-materiality of Christian Science is anomalous, for the rest of the system does not accept and practise the non-materiality of life. The separation of one part of experience, that having to do with illness and health, from the rest of human experience causes a dangerous bifurcation of life.

However, the non-materiality of Christian Science is an understandable reaction against the unreasonable materialism of much of medical thought and practice. The evidence accumulated by Christian Science practice cannot be ignored in seeking an understanding of the total nature of man and his health as a form of behaviour. But we must move well beyond its irrational philosophy, its intolerant practice, and its bifurcation of experience in order to understand the varied factors at work in creating disease and in restoring wholeness of being.

The development of sound methods of healing do not come from a petulant effort at protecting small areas of truth that can be verified by limited experience. It does come from a willingness to examine the complicated experience of man in his complex life so that a careful analysis of varied experience can become the solid basis for the type of synthesis that makes room for all the truth there is in illuminating man's nature and his behaviour.

Science is built on the ability of the human mind to classify experience and clarify its meaning through the adequacy of its

classification. The same process is important in categorizing the behaviour that shows up in illness and health.

If psychosomatic research shows the importance of the person, it is also significant that other predictable factors are at work to affect sickness and health.

4

The Person behind the Disease

Disease is a matter of disordered function or organic breakdown in an individual. There is no such thing as a group disease. It is always a matter of an individual. Large numbers of persons in any given group may be subject to disease, and often the same disease. But even in epidemic conditions, the course of the disease varies with different people. The physician and the nurse, because of some condition that seems prevalent among them, may escape the illness. Some may have it in light form while others die of it. Even in an epidemic, individual characteristics are noted. If that is so under such widely spread group conditions, how much more so would individual characteristics determine the course of disease or the freedom from it when no epidemic existed.

Aetiology is the study of cause. In understanding disease it is important to know the causative elements. We see cause-and-effect relations at work. Medicine has always sought to understand disease by understanding its cause. The history of medicine has employed differing methods for determining these causes. Aristotle and Galen thought of illness as disturbances of the elements and humours. They treated the whole being rather than individual parts. Chaucer characterized the physician of his time in these apt words:

> He knew the cause of every malady
> Where it is hot, or cold, or moist or dry;
> And where engendered, and of what humour.
> He was a very perfect practiser.

Modern science has been preoccupied with mechanics and applied physics. Medicine in the last century or two has concentrated more and more on the mechanical parts and their interaction than upon the total being. The individual has been treated as an accumulation of parts which need fuel, lubrication and adjustment to keep functioning. When function breaks down, an effort is made to determine the offending part, and restore it to proper operation. This may involve modifying the body chemistry through medicine, or a more drastic approach to the offending part through surgical intervention. This has led to specialization, where physicians develop more and more knowledge about the function of individual parts of the total being. Such an approach has naturally moved away from a concern for the total individual. In this process, certain knowledge of the total functioning of man has been lost in a preoccupation with the mechanical view of the parts. As T. S. Eliot has put it, 'Where is the knowledge we have lost in information?'

Within recent decades a new concern for preventive medicine and a new interest in the non-material nature of reality has led research beyond the mechanical concern for parts, which is essentially curative, to an understanding or an effort to understand the causative factors as a product of the total response of the total individual to the total process of living.

This has led towards a new and active interest in the place of the emotions in the aetiology of disease. The result of this shift of emphasis has produced interesting historical conflicts. Major attention was directed toward the medical, dental and therapeutic use of hypnosis in the late nineteenth century. Bitter conflict arose as to the soundness of such a direct approach to the lower levels of consciousness of the patient. Although it was effective in symptom removal, it was largely abandoned as a sole form of therapy because what appeared to be symptom removal was more accurately described as symptom displacement. The removal of the symptom of an emotional state without correcting the basic cause led to the appearance of other symptoms that were as dangerous as the original state.

One of the early interests of Freud was the euphoric effect of

cocaine. His liberal use of the drug before the more damaging effects were ascertained has its modern counterpart in the widespread use of 'tranquillizers', which appear to have a more widespread and subtle danger for mankind than the more obvious dangers of cocaine.

These efforts to use drugs or chemical agents to help bring about a more desirable state of emotions was a clear recognition of the awareness of the emotional factor in illness. The mechanical or surgical intervention in such conditions is found in electric shock therapy and lobotomies. Here again, the total health of the individual is approached by an intervention of a type and fashion designed to re-establish balance in the whole through an act directed towards one part.

Modern medical practice has been engaged in a major conflict between the ideas of the organicists and those who are more concerned with emotional and functional aetiology. Yet the more research is done, the more it seems apparent that the total being is involved in every diseased state, and all specialization ultimately has to face the fact that there is no physical state that is not affected by emotion, and no emotion that does not have its effect on the physical state. In fact, they are so inseparably bound together that it is difficult to tell where one ends and the other begins. It is as difficult to tell which comes first as the chicken or the egg. Ultimately they always come together.

Recent study of virus shows that the same virus can cause leukaemia in some patients and mononucleosis in others, depending on the emotional state of the individual. Stress creates chemical reactions that reduce protection against abnormal cell division. The emotions make the difference.

Something about the individual in each instance is of such importance that he has to be the primary consideration in dealing with any disease-state that happens to him. The variations in aging, in response to environment and stress factors, in the proneness to accident and the involvement of emotional factors, are all individual. Immunity, susceptibility, even the cell structure of an individual are the primary data of illness and health. Any approach to the problems of illness and health,

then, would have to be concerned not so much with the body as with the trinity of body, mind and spirit.

The individual and the aging process

The passing of time may have differing effects on different persons. What we usually speak of as aging is governed by at least four major factors and a number of minor ones. Aging is subject to natural laws, and the cycle of birth, growth, withering and death is observed in nature in one form or another with all forms of organized energy. It may be the millions of years before the radiant energy of the atom of radium ages into the atom of lead, or it may be the few hours of a day in which a fragile moth leaves the cocoon, lays its eggs and dies. The natural process of organic response to the passing of time is everywhere observable. Man does not escape the basic laws of life to which he is subject along with the rest of nature.

But in man there are other forces at work to hasten or retard the process. Persons living in the same climate, eating much the same diet and participating in the same life processes have varying rate of physical aging. As Cecil G. Sheps has made clear, 'Aging and disease are different processes. From the biological point of view aging is a natural condition. It starts before birth at the moment of conception and goes on throughout life.' Even within the person there are varying rates of aging going on. Some cells in the nervous system last the lifetime of the individual and others are being continually replaced with a life span of three or four days. 'No individual is of the same biologic age throughout. A person may have a cardiovascular system equivalent to the average of forty-year olds and a digestive system characteristic of sixty-five-year olds.'

No one knows what the prime of life is. Sprint records are usually made by persons about twenty years of age, but the marathon runs are won by men around forty. Age involves changes, varied abilities, important compensations and valuable experiences.

As muscular vigour and speed decreases, co-ordinating skills often increase. Aging reduces the tolerance of some people to drugs, and increases that of others. Nutritional needs also change. There is, for example, a reduction of caloric requirements but an increased need for calcium and protein.

Even the types of disease vary with age. Young persons tend to suffer from acute diseases while the aged are afflicted with chronic disease. And the causes of death change from generation to generation depending on environmental factors.

In 1900 the five leading causes of death were, in this order, pneumonia, tuberculosis, diarrhoea, heart disease and kidney disease. Now they are heart disease, cancer, deaths by violence, apoplexy, and kidney disease. . . In 1900, chronic illness was responsible for approximately half the deaths. Now it is responsible for 60 per cent of all disability and for 80 per cent of the deaths.

So four-fifths of deaths today are terminal events from long-standing chronic illness. This makes for difficulty in treatment, for causative factors and diagnosis are approached with limited understanding.

The disease is often considerably advanced before symptoms occur, thus making for delay in discovery and diagnosis. In youth, the cause of disease is usually acute, self-limited, brief, immunizing, with little individual variation. In senescence, the cause is usually chronic rather than immunizing; it often produces increased vulnerability to other diseases. It is progressive and there is very wide individual variation. This produces long-lasting disability prior to death.

Medical knowledge is severely limited and therapeutic procedures are inadequate.

As a matter of fact, we are particularly bad in combating the so-called degenerative diseases among males over the age of forty-five, and also accidents among both sexes.

What we know about the physiological details of aging is surrounded by an ocean of our ignorance.

There is far too little research on the whole man – his individual psychology and its reaction to the way he lives his life – in relation to his future cardiac health or disease. Before heart disease is discoverable, individuals can differ in their mode of life and in every morphological, biochemical, physiological, and social characteristic we can measure. It is reasonable to expect that these individual differences in the healthy state are related to great differences in the eventual appearance of or freedom from heart disease. . . Prevention must be the keynote and hope, but so far there is extremely little to offer because almost nothing is known of the pre-disease personal characteristics, or the life-long habits, or the factors of diet, or exercise, of emotion, of physical and social environment, of other illnesses and accidents far removed in time, which make one man a candidate for early death and give his fellow man relative immunity.[1]

While certain types of physical disability appear to increase with the aging process, we see many older persons who enjoy excellent health. The natural progression of life does not necessarily carry with it the aches, pains and groans that many acquire. Our knowledge of the physiological aspects of aging gives us but slight clues as to what happens to the whole man with the passing of time.

An important social factor must be considered in the behaviour of the aging. In some Mediterranean countries the useful role of women is considered to be over when the children reach maturity. Many women accept the idea that they are old at forty and look and act as they picture themselves to be. Women of similar background in a different culture adopt the ideas and attitudes of their surroundings and so retard the evidences of the aging process.

This social factor is observed in reactions to retirement. Many persons live full and useful lives until the time of retirement and then deteriorate rapidly. It has been noted that

many persons die within six months of retirement. The feeling that they do not serve a socially useful function, plus the fact that there is no life-sustaining routine or interest, causes life to fall apart at the seams. Yet many persons whose retirement is a prelude to another interesting and useful phase of living go on for years enjoying health and well-being.

Many of the physical indispositions of the aged appear to be not so much a form of physical disorganization as they are social and psychological disintegration. This is borne out by research on the mental health of the aged. It has been an easy practice to attribute signs of disintegration among the aged to arteriosclerotic brain disease or to so-called senile dementia. Competent investigators have demonstrated, however, that neither of the two clinical diagnoses is often confirmed by post-mortem gross or microscopic examination of the brain. The symptoms that often lead to a diagnosis which assumes physiological breakdown may be the result of loss of interest in life and a gradual withdrawal from meaningful living.

While little coordinated research into the nature of personality response to the aging process has been done, there is a large body of evidence that sustains the idea that aging can be retarded by favourable conditions of mind and environment. A physician tells me of two hypochondriacal sisters who had long harassed him with their ailments. Almost facetiously he asked, 'Why don't you learn Spanish? It would be good for you.' They did, and started a new era in their lives with new friends, new experiences and travel in Latin countries. Their ailments disappeared and they enjoyed the best years of their lives, physically, mentally and emotionally.

This sort of thing is not an uncommon occurrence for those practising medicine to observe. Those who are not in the medical practice are also aware of it. An old lady of about eighty was becoming erratic in her behaviour, and neighbours asked the minister to see if he could do something to protect her from herself. He arranged for a medical examination in the county hospital, and a week later was greeted by these words from the physician: 'Your old lady will be all right when we get her

sobered up and the alcohol out of her system.' Although she had never taken a drink until the year before, she had not been really sober for nearly a year. But a place in a home for persons her age with new interests and proper care restored her to more normal behaviour.

Much of what happens to persons with the passing of years is a product of inter-related conditions. Proper diet and stimulating living conditions, a healthful philosophy of life and a creative attitude of mind can do much to give health and vitality to the years. The absence of such advantageous conditions may hasten deterioration of body, mind and spirit. More than we have ever dared to think, the advancing years can be made spiritually productive in such a way that all of life is made more satisfying. Aging is not so much a measuring of the passing of time as it is a loss of some vital spiritual capacity that values life.

Certain physiological conditions can be traced, but there is no fixed law governing the physiological changes of all persons. Other conditions are at work to modify the passing of the years. The attitude towards the older person in any given society appears to have a definite bearing on the health and well-being of its older members. The psychological conditions that have to do with how one looks at one's own life age-wise are also important. The person who thinks he is old is apt to be. The person who thinks young, who enjoys new interests and young ideas, keeps something of eternal youth about him.

Though the aging process may have some bearing on the general health of the individual, there are no diseases that appear to afflict only the aged. There are no limits to the good health and joy of living that can be shared by older persons if the internal and external conditions sustain it. And no one need die of disease. The process of dying may be the fitting end of a natural process where the person who has fruitfully completed his span of years may 'wrap the draperies of his couch about him and lie down to pleasant dreams'.

Science is doing strange things with the theory of time. It is not now viewed as the abstract construction to suit the convenience of men's minds, but is rather an imponderable dimen-

sion of the creative process. The mind that shares the creative attitude seems to be able to dart in and out of time, and the phenomena of the precognitive mental activity give substance to this conjecture about some power that gives mastery even over time. If this is true of mental activity of a limited type, it may be possible for us to foresee the time when disciplined minds may even 'take a tuck in time' and find that quality of being that Ponce DeLeon sought so persistently. It may well be that the surmising soul is reaching out towards that state of being where the creative power of mind is master of those measurements that have long been considered to exist only for its convenience.

As science becomes more adept in dealing with those aspects of existence that are less materialistic and more akin to the spiritual, it may give further verification to the philosophical judgment of Santayana who said, 'Nothing is inherently and invincibly young except spirit. And spirit can enter a human being perhaps better in the quiet of old age and dwell there more undisturbed than in the turmoil of adventure.' Perhaps the only question one would ask in response to such a statement is, 'Who better than Santayana knew the meaning of spiritual adventure?'

The individual and his environment

The study of psychosocial medicine has become a special interest only recently. While men have always known there was some relationship between environment and health, they have not pursued it scientifically until the interest in psychosomatic medicine stimulated its correlative study of the effect of the external surroundings on the internal response.

Much that we now take for granted has had an effect upon health. Gradual modification of life from primitive times has made indistinct some of the major health influences.

When primitive man was a nomad he had no problem of garbage disposal or elementary sanitation. When men came together in cities they sought security in numbers against

enemies. But the enemies that were controlled on one hand were equalled by the enemies that were created on the other, and plagues, group fears, and problems of sanitation were long to be a serious health problem to mankind. In mediaeval times, cities were known by their smells, and many persons, prominent as well as impoverished, suffered from the effects of filth. In Italy herds of pigs were driven along the streets to act as scavengers and eat the refuse that was thrown from doors and windows. Only within the last hundred years has there been any understanding of the health danger of filth, and a well-designed programme of sanitary controls has been instituted. For centuries this part of man's environment was a major health factor.

So also, nutrition has been an important environmental condition. Primitive man ate raw food. The supply was not certain and the quality and quantity varied. When men came together to live in cities they suffered for want of food, and not only was the quality of food changed but its status as a weapon was used. Enemies had only to set fire to the wheat fields surrounding a city to bring its inhabitants to starvation and subjection. Modern agriculture has increased the supply of food, but chemical agents used for fertilizers and pest controls have brought with them another type of health hazard.

When men lived in caves they had no control over the air of their dwellings. In temperate and colder climates ventilation was always second to the need for warmth. Only with recent times has there been central heating, air-conditioning and controlled ventilation. This, too, has had a bearing on the health of men, for the inadequate oxygen content of air produced weakened bodily states and reduced resistance to those external conditions that affected the body's function.

The atmosphere surrounding a city can have its effect upon the well-being of its inhabitants. Smoke, smog and other irritants tend to affect the systems of individuals in varying degrees. Also, increases in the radiation count in the outer atmosphere with the accompanying fall out are environmental factors that are currently affecting health.

Employment is a factor in environment. Not only are there

direct health factors involved, such as in mining and deep-sea diving, or working in high-pressure tunnels, but the monotony, interest factor, or surroundings of the worker have a direct bearing on the emotional health of the individual. The frustration factor in employment creates the kind of stress that shows itself in physical symptoms.

In a society that has endured major world wars at the rate of one a generation, it is inevitable that this aspect of our modern environment would be examined. The violent death of millions of soldiers and civilians is matched by the conditions of stress that make inroads upon the health of millions of others.

But when all is said that can be said about the many external conditions that are continually playing upon the lives of individuals, we cannot ignore the qualities of individuals that determine how the environment reacts upon the individual. What Dr Dunbar speaks of as 'the personality profile' has a direct bearing upon the way persons react to environment. The same external conditions play upon the soldier who is brought low with shell shock or battle fatigue as upon one who goes through campaign after campaign without serious emotional injury. The businessman under stress develops physical symptoms that are damaging while his colleague with much the same type of stress appears to have no such reactions.

Here again, what we know about the relationship of the external and the internal is surrounded by so much that we do not know that we are feeling our way towards some insights that may be useful in the future. But when we face the reactions of certain individuals and groups of individuals to disease, we also have to understand why it is that other individuals under similar circumstances do not react with the kind of behaviour that we speak of as breakdown and illness.

It was Jesus who declared that 'it is not what goes into the body that defiles it, but what cometh from it'. It is not so much the environment as the internal conditions upon which the environment plays that lead to disintegration and collapse.

What we are beginning to learn about the importance of man's spiritual nature as a creative and determining force in

the shaping of his reaction to all else in life cannot be overlooked here. A man with limited diet, limited environment and limited social resources but an integrated and powerful spirit can change history. A well-fed, privileged and prominent individual with a crippled or infantile spirit can come and go with no discernible ripple on the surface of history. The comparison of Jesus and Pontius Pilate makes such a contrast too emphatic.

It is in that direction that we must move if we are to grasp the important 'X factor' at work to place the mark of great destiny where it seems strangely inexplicable. The internal power of a charged spirit bears fruit this world hardly dreams of.

The individual and accident

To the average person an accident is an accident. It is usually considered to be the unfortunate confluence of man and the immutable forces of natural law. In fact, often such circumstances are legally referred to as 'acts of God'.

Recent statistical studies are making us aware of the fact that there is a clear profile of the accident-prone, and in industry and on the highways a large percentage of the accidents involve a small percentage of the people. Therefore, it begins to appear that accidents are a type of behaviour with a disguised motive. The person who commits the accident is satisfying needs that cannot be easily satisfied in other ways.

We are just beginning to find out many things about accidents. There are at least four classifications into which they may fall. First is the accident that is consciously planned, but the motivation is concealed from all but the planner. Second is the accident that is unconsciously planned. Third is the accident that is explained by no conscious or unconscious motivation in the individual, though a certain amount of preknowledge indicates that there was some other force than mere happenstance; and fourth, the pure accident, so called, because we find no other explanation and no explanation seems reasonable.

Insurance companies suspect that certain accidents involving automobile deaths are deliberately planned suicide attempts

disguised so that beneficiaries will be able to cash in on the double indemnity clauses of their insurance. During the war a rash of minor self-inflicted wounds occurred with the obvious purpose of getting an extra five points toward the total required for return to the Continental United States, not to speak of the attractive Purple Heart. So also self-inflicted wounds were a type of life insurance under battle conditions. The consciously planned accident is nothing more than an attempt at deception for personal reasons.

The unconsciously planned accident is just as much a hazard, though the motivation may be more obscure. It may be a form of self-inflicted injury due to anger turned in upon the self. Self-mutilation and guilt are often related in the unconscious mind.

The State of Connecticut has employed a psychiatrist to examine persons involved in automobile accidents on its Merritt Parkway. A large percentage of the persons involved in accidents have been in a state of anger preceding the accident. When this anger is directed against the self it creates the mood of carelessness and recklessness that produces accidents. Many of the persons interviewed saw no connection between their emotional state and what happened to them, but the behaviour mechanisms that were operative did not depend upon a conscious awareness for effectiveness.

It is well known that aggressive feelings, when suppressed, may be turned against the self or others in a form of action that is so camouflaged that the person committing the acts is unaware of their meaning. This kind of suppressed aggression is the stuff the unconscious accident is made of.

Also, states of depression with their accompanying lassitude and carelessness resemble the kind of fatigue that is accident-producing. Damaged emotional states are continually producing the conditions that unconsciously direct energy in destructive channels. Whether it is lassitude or an aggressive feeling, the results produced, when sifted through the mechanisms of the unconscious, are the accidents that fulfil the needs of

individuals in spite of the conscious controls they would tend to employ.

The third type of accident is more difficult to deal with because of the subtle nature of the psychic factors involved. However, enough is known of such things to make it reasonable to conjecture that more exists than meets the eye. Sometimes persons indicate a strange feeling that something is going to happen. When it happens, the foreknowledge modifies its purely accidental nature, though to the individuals involved, the causative factors appear to be unknown.

An Air Force Captain came to me during the Second World War and described an experience of precognition. He asked what its meaning might be. His training in applied science gave no basis for interpreting such mental phenomena, though he said it was one of the most real things that had ever happened to him. He described in detail as to time, place and circumstances the crashing of his plane later that day. He described the feelings surrounding his own death. Later that day, at the time and place indicated, the plane crashed and he was killed, though he was not then at the controls. The mathematical possibility of chance, considering the large number of verifiable facts, would be astronomical, and beyond reasonable consideration. Two alternative explanations remain. The first is that a death wish, so strong that it could have been compelling, might have been a factor, but this does not seem reasonable as an explanation when the officer in question was not at the controls. The other alternative appears to be some psychic factor that foresaw the events, but was unable to control them. This is beyond the range of the purely accidental, for forewarning is a predisposing factor against the accidental. It appears, then, that in some circumstances, psychic or perhaps superconscious forces are at work beyond the control or understanding of the persons who are enmeshed in them.

An increase in our understanding of psychic phenomena may well throw light on many of those circumstances we have until now considered to be purely accidental.

The pure accident is the category into which we place all

happenstances for which no conscious, unconscious or psychic motivation is known. This category may well be whittled away as we get to know more of the ways the consciousness employs to achieve its purposes. Here elements of sensitivity and awareness, or the lack of them, may be as significant as the fact that even in the midst of an epidemic certain persons are free from disease, though subject to the same exposure as others.

Here a careful study of the insights of primitive peoples may reveal to anthropologists the movement of mind and emotion into realms we little understand and of which we are completely unaware. In the world of pure physics there is more place now for pattern and design, and less place for chance. It would be unreasonable to eliminate the life of man with his higher levels of adjustment from the type of law and order that works in all the rest of creation. The patterns and designs may be more complex, but this should not lead us to ignore them, even though their elusiveness may for a long time perplex us.

The individual and his emotions

Having recognized the aging process, the effect of the encroaching environment, and the impact of the accidental upon man and his physical well-being, we come now to the subject-matter that will engage our attention throughout the rest of this book, the relation of mind, emotion, thought and feeling to the physical well-being of man.

These inner factors exerting an influence on the health of a man may be as simple as the basic attitude of a person towards life itself. If a person approaches each day with dread, and is afraid to get out of bed in the morning for fear of what the day will do to him, he is certainly in a much more susceptible mood for harbouring any disease than the person who enjoys life and enters each day's activity with enthusiasm and enjoyment.

Apprehension about life that is continually seeking escape would easily adapt itself to the privileged status given to the sick in our society.

The punishment of life for real or neurotic guilt may readily

show itself through the channels of disease. The increased awareness of the causes of psychogenic illness is bound to increase the sense of guilt among those who are close to such persons, and in turn spread wider the evidences of man's use of illness as a form of self-punishment.

The physician in working with persons is aware of the complicated nature of the being he deals with. The less adventurous and less perceptive try to simplify the patient to mechanics or chemistry, but their number is becoming less as the overpowering evidence of man's complicated involvement in health is revealed. As one physician said to me, 'Aside from the stopping of the flow of blood, and the giving of antibiotics in dealing with certain infections, medical practice is just what it is called, a practice, seeking to make perfect, but always aware of its experimental nature.' Yet even here the personal variables cannot be ignored, for the coagulative factor in the blood of one person is quite different from that of another, and the antibiotic that is effective with one person tends to poison another.

The studies of Jerome Frank at Johns Hopkins mentioned earlier point out that the role of the physician in the practice of the healing arts may be far more dependent upon the suggestion implied in his presence, and the faith inspired by his training, than even he accepts.

It is at this point that the suggestion implicit in the role of the clergyman may supplement the suggestion made by the role of the physician, especially if there is a sympathetic and co-operative understanding between the two disciplines. The basic assumptions of religion that health is good, and illness is not good, may become the basis for the kind of suggestion that can move the person away from the mood of illness towards the acceptance of more constructive ways of dealing with stress. It is at this point that the function of faith as a major life orientation, and the use of prayer as a form of specialized thinking about life, have traditionally played a therapeutic part and may now do so more effectively.

Both religion and science have been guilty of errors in dealing with the phenomena of health. Sometimes religion has tended

to ignore the physical realities in favour of the spiritual. At other times science has so concentrated on the material that it has lost sight of a spiritual pattern at work in life. Now it is possible through new insights of both science and religion to move beyond these errors and lay hold of more effective ways of dealing with the causative factors in illness. This does not become an escape from reality, but rather a more adequate means of dealing with a larger reality.

The elements of inner balance

Nature is busily at work to assist the physical organism in maintaining the kind of balance that leads to effective living. A process of inner repair is continually at work to restrain the aging process. An ability to adapt and adjust is constantly modifying the impact of the environment on the individual. Even in relation to accidents, the reflex actions of the organism are continually saving the individual from many of the injuries towards which his subconscious mind may be impelling him. And the emotions of man are continually being soothed by time and the adaptive process, so that persons go through the most harrowing experiences with more aplomb than they would have imagined possible.

Hans Selye has pointed out the effect of stress in organic breakdown. It is equally important to point out the variety of ways in which the organism is adapting itself to pressures from without and within.

Walter B. Cannon, in his book *The Wisdom of the Body*, has pointed out the variety of ways in which the body adapts itself to the forces that work on it. Taking the various organs, glands and the blood he portrays the various ways by which the adaptive processes of homeostasis take place.

Lawrence LeShan, writing in the *Journal of the American Cancer Society*, shows a comparable factor at work at the point of achieving intropsychic balance. Here, in an effort to establish what takes place in 'spontaneous regressions' of malignancies, a series of experiments in deep analysis of patients suffering

from inoperable cancer shows a modification of the malignancy as the intropsychic balance was restored.[2]

It is not unreasonable to believe and demonstrate in practice that a comparable spiritual equilibrium may have an important contribution to make to the understanding of illness and health. It is to that task, then, that we would set ourselves.[3]

5

Health as an Affirmation of Life

It is an accepted fact that all behaviour is full of meaning. Often the meaning is disguised. At other times we work hard to keep from facing the meaning of our behaviour. But the insight we have into how people function makes it increasingly difficult to deny that our behaviour is purposive.

One of the places where we are apt to resist this insight about our behaviour is in matters of health. We are slow to admit that illness and health are types of behaviour with a purpose.

The reasons for this are simple. We have been brought up in a culture where illness and health are major concerns. From early years the physician is an important person in our lives. We receive special consideration when we are ill. In fact, ours is a culture that guarantees certain rewards for ill health. When do we receive flowers? When do we have breakfast in bed? When are we told not to worry about our work? Not usually when we are well.

However, some important developments in recent years have been affecting this attitude towards health. We are being compelled to take a long and careful look at the nature of man, the sources of ill-health and the ways to health and wholeness.

These compelling forces come from research in carefully defined fields of science. So much has been happening that it is not easy to keep the old boundaries intact. Combinations of various branches of science that would have been strange indeed a generation ago are now commonplace, and we speak of bio-physics and astro-physics without batting an eye. And so

psychology affects medicine, and physics affects biology, and all of them help to illuminate this complicated being we call man.

Let us look first at what psychology has to say that contributes to the changing picture of man's attitude toward illness and health. Our first response to the idea that our health is a form of behaviour is apt to be, 'Nonsense! It is foolish to think anyone would want to be sick.' To this, psychology would say, 'It is not a simple matter. The desire to be well is strong, but the unconscious needs of the person can be strong also. This conflict can lead to organic breakdown and illness.'

It is a common experience for the organic response to a conflict to show up as a cold. A check of a high school during an examination week in June found that more than half of the students taking certain examinations had colds on the day of the exam, and that the colds seemed to appear simultaneously. The students wanted to be at their best but they had a fear of failure and a deep desire to escape from the ordeal.

In more spectacular form the same principle is at work in a military replacement centre where men are reassigned for combat missions. The desire to do one's duty and be brave is in conflict with a fear of pain and death. The result may be physical paralysis in the form of blindness, lameness or backache, symptoms produced by the emotions. The psychologist calls this conversion hysteria, a state of being where deep feelings are turned into physical manifestations in order to resolve an inner conflict.

The psychologist can add a long list of such responses to life which explain the behaviour we call illness.

The physiologist also has something important to say at this point. He studies the living, active organism as a whole. He tries to understand the connections of one part with the other.

So it was that Lord Adrian, the British Nobel Prize winner, studied the relation of mind and body. He found that the ten thousand million specialized cells that make up the human brain can be modified by the way in which they are used. In quiet, relaxed states of mind the surface of these cells remains

smooth. However, in intense thought or concentration, as in working on a problem or engaging in prayer, the cells are modified. The outer surface becomes wrinkled. In this process molecules are projected through the surface of the cells and a measurable amount of electricity is generated. So, thought focused on a part of the body can actually stimulate a type of cellular response that is communicated from the brain to the part of the body involved.

The response of our built-in electrical control system is a familiar experience. We think about biting into a lemon and our salivary glands begin to secrete. We intensify our thought about one of our hands, and before long we can begin to feel the blood pulsing through it and it becomes increasingly sensitive to a variety of sensations that are not usually felt.

If this is true of our response to deliberate efforts, we can well imagine how the physiologist would observe the responses to deep and unconscious mental activity, especially if it is stimulated by strong emotion. When a person is embarrassed, he does not consciously say to himself, 'Now is the time for me to blush.' Usually the person communicates his embarrassment by his behaviour, which in this instance is visible to another who may say, 'You are blushing'. It is not difficult to see how behaviour is continually being conditioned by our thoughts and feelings at many levels of our being, if this principle of relationship is so clearly obvious in a superficial way.

The insights of the psychologist and the physiologist are amplified by the practical observations of the physician who is exploring the relation of mind, body and emotion, or the branch of medicine we call psychosomatics. Phenomena in this field have long been observed, but more recently have been correlated and understood.

Physicians are aware of a phenomenon that must be just as flattering in one way as it is annoying in another. A physician is often called to minister to the needs of a patient in acute discomfort, and on arriving finds that the patient is much better. The patient will say, 'I am sorry to have bothered you at this time of night, but as soon as I called you I felt better.' The

knowledge that help was coming relieved anxiety and the relief of anxiety had an immediate physical reaction.

It is not uncommon for patients in post-surgical discomfort to be given injections of distilled water instead of morphine. And the result is often expressed in an appreciative glance at the nurse and the words, 'Thanks, now I can go to sleep.' And the patient soon falls into a restful sleep in response to an idea that is injected into his being via the hypodermic needle.

Estimates vary as to the amount of illness that grows from mental and emotional causes, but a paper read at the national convention of the American Medical Association in 1956 said that one hundred per cent of illness is psychosomatic in the sense that there is no physical condition to which the emotions do not respond, and no emotional condition that does not leave its mark on the physical organism.[1] In the last fifteen or twenty years a major change in the climate of medical practice has been brought about by the new insights that are emerging from studies in this field.

The skilful and perceptive explorations of psychosomatics by members of the medical profession are illuminating the nature of man and his functioning so that a new idea of health and wholeness is emerging.

It was long felt that the physical sciences were remote from the study of man himself, but now that does not seem to be the case.

The physical sciences have not only given us a completely new idea of matter, but they have indicated something important about the forces that are continually at work to change and modify the state of matter. In the *Midcentury Survey of Medical Research* it is pointed out that electronic factors involving the physical organism are a major field of modern research, for the change in the state of one molecule can start a chain reaction that can involve the whole body. If this is true, it is clear that small, obscure factors can be of great importance to the total health of a human being.

The study of electronics and radiation not only serves a useful purpose diagnostically, but also helps to show how the system

responds to a variety of stimuli. This leads to a careful study of the mysterious power that has been referred to as 'the healing force'. There was a time when such a belief was ridiculed as a fraud of the witch doctors or the product of a diseased imagination. In recent years Julius Weinberger, a physicist doing research for RCA, has been able to isolate and identify a measurable radiation passing from the hands of a praying clergyman into the body of a person being prayed for during the ancient rite known as the laying on of hands. If the change in the state of one molecule can start a chain reaction modifying the condition of the whole body, such a phenomenon during the laying on of hands has a new significance for those interested in isolating the healing force.

Studies in parapsychology carry such research a step further by demonstrating certain powers of the mind to project energy in intelligible form so that communication takes place without the usual sensory stimuli. Some scientists react against this idea as vigorously as the colleagues of Madam Curie reacted against her idea of a radioactive element. But the facts of para-psychological research are no longer a matter of debate. The problem now is, what does it mean?

From the point of view of man's health and wholeness, the findings of the parapsychologists verify the fact that there is a way of relating the mind of one person to the mind of another, either for good or ill. In distressing conditions, anxiety can be communicated. In more favourable states of mind, such as prayer, it seems logical to such men as the late Alexis Carrell, research director for the Rockefeller Medical Foundation, that a healing force can be communicated.

Such insights from psychology, physiology, psychosomatic medicine, physics and parapsychology have forced the exponents of religious practice to re-examine the relation of religion to health. This has led to three major types of reaction among those who are interested in the problems of religion and the healing force.

First, there are those who, with uncritical exuberance, make exaggerated claims. Through mass suggestion and melodra-

matic atmosphere an appeal is made to strong emotions, often with quite spectacular results. This approach, although made in the name of religion, does not seem to show an adequate respect for the nature of human personality, and tends to trifle with the sacred feelings of people. While some good is done, there is a grave danger that such an assault affects only the symptoms leaving the underlying causes untouched. A careful evaluation is difficult because usually neither the healers nor the patients are interested in supplying documentary data. While it is important to study the approach of such 'spiritual healers', it may well be that their methods jeopardize real progress.

Second, many men in the field of religion feel that the implications of these new insights into the nature of man and his health are so complicated and far-reaching that it is danger-ous to become involved in any way. They fear a threat to their traditional theology. This *laissez-faire* attitude says in effect, 'Hands off. We leave health to the physician. We teach religion pure and simple.' Such a cautious approach denies a major aspect of religious practice, for religion has always been con-cerned with the wholeness of its communicants.

A third reaction, and the one which engages us in this book, is the desire to bring the clearest and most courageous religious insights into accord with other branches of thought as we explore the power of religion to produce wholeness and health. The importance to religion of the findings of psychosomatic medicine and other correlated sciences is tremendous.

Dr James Nickson, director of radiological research at Mem-orial Hospital in New York says, 'Life, like a diamond, has many facets. Medical science with its researches and its limi-tations can throw a certain type of light on life. But there are many other facets with their types of light. They must all be brought together to add to our understanding of man and his health.'

In his study of *The Healing Cults*, Louis S. Reed MD sums up his feeling as follows:

In religious healing, particularly where states of religious exaltation are involved, it must be evident that the suggestion of health or cure is linked with and made dynamic by a complex of ideas and emotions of tremendous power. Quite possibly religious healing makes use of forces not ordinarily recognized. . .[2]

The religious approach is not concerned primarily with the treatment of symptoms but with the achievement of spiritual unity which produces wholeness of being. The insight that can be shed upon man's total health from an understanding of his spiritual nature and its processes is tremendous.

Health is not merely an absence of illness. It is a dynamic, positive response to life, the fruit of an inner balance that produces and maintains wholeness. Religion is the major contributive factor to the integrity of being that produces such a response.

Illness as a loss of faith in life

Illness is a morbid state of being. It is a life-destroying condition. In industry reference is made to 'days lost due to illness'. As a simple mathematical fact, days lost from life are a form of denial of life, and if all behaviour is purposeful, then it is important to examine the conditions that lead people to forfeit life in return for the benefits of illness.

When the burdens of life and the pain of existence become so acute that they produce a state of depression, a person may destroy himself. Such a capitulation to intolerable stress is emotional illness in an extreme form. The will to die overpowers the will to live.

In less extreme form, life is denied or destroyed a little at a time in return for benefits that seem sufficient for the person who is ill. Yet usually the person engaged in this self-destructive behaviour is slow to admit it, for the needs to be satisfied are important to the total scheme of his life.

If we understand alcohol addiction as a form of ill-health, we

can see how the process works. Life becomes painful and the problems of life too difficult to handle easily. Alcohol serves as a self-administered form of psychotherapy in two ways. It tends to relieve the suffering at the same time that it creates the feeling of adequacy and competence. The realization that the relief from the pain is temporary and that the feeling of competence is illusory creates more discomfort and an increased need for relief. So the problem is self-aggravating. Too often only the symptoms are treated, rather than the deep psychological causes. Sometimes the cause of self-destructive behaviour can be reached at the conscious level, but often the roots are deeply concealed and have to be dealt with at the unconscious level.

The unconscious roots of destructive behaviour

With the alcoholic the compulsion to drink may not be related to a conscious need. Deep in his unconscious mind there may be an emotional echo of a condition in his early life. When he was hungry, he felt pain. When he cried, he was fed and the pain subsided. The unconscious pattern that relates inner pain with oral satisfaction may be so strong in him that under conditions of great stress he reverts to the earlier pattern for relieving pain and discomfort. The pain of his adult years may be psychic, rather than the physical pain caused by hunger contractions. However, such distinctions seem to be lost to the lower levels of consciousness, and the compulsion towards satisfaction is so strong that he cannot easily resist it, even though he may be aware of its self-destructive effect upon his life when he consciously deliberates the matter.

Such unconscious factors may show themselves in other types of illness where the connections may not be so clearly established. Such was the case with Mrs R, who had a long history of what was referred to as 'female troubles'. As a girl, Mrs R was brought up in a brutally strict and misguided Victorian atmosphere. Anything having to do with sex or the bearing of children was considered to be too revolting for words. The onset of menstruation was referred to as a calamity, the arrival of 'the

curse'. Her mind was filled with every possible morbid suggestion on the subject, if not directly, more effectively by indirection. She was led to believe that men were loathsome brutes, to
be tolerated as a necessary evil but never to be encouraged.
From the point of view of mental conditioning her life was a
chamber of emotional horrors.

It is not strange, then, that the physical equipment of Mrs R,
which is highly responsive to emotional stimulus, should have
caused her great difficulty. For years her menstrual period was
accompanied with acute pain because of contractions due to
anxiety and fear. When the pain become intolerable, it was
blotted out by the temporary expedient of a fainting spell. Her
married life was characterized by fear, suspicion and persistent
illness. Her one pregnancy was complicated. She was hospital-
ized three times during its course, and had a long and painful
delivery. Continued ill-health and a series of minor operations
finally led to a surgically induced menopause which was complicated by emotional disturbance that involved psychotherapy.
From this she emerged with an improved state of health and a
mood of general well-being.

It would have been difficult for Mrs R at any point in her
history of physical disturbance to have accepted the fact that
her condition was self-destructive behaviour unconsciously
caused. Had she received psychotherapy earlier, the problems
might have been resolved. However, it is not difficult to see that
the highly charged emotional conditioning early in her life made
her fearful of any of the manifestations of her role as a woman.
A variety of physical symptoms gave evidence of the power of
these feelings through many years, and finally led to the
destruction of those organic parts of her being that identified
her as a woman. While none of her behaviour was a conscious
response, there is little doubt that her illness was a form of
response of life, caused by deep unconscious disturbances of the
emotions.

More than we are apt to realize, the medical case-histories of
many persons reveal the dynamic factors at work in the lower

levels of consciousness to produce a type of behaviour whose symptoms we identify as illness or disease.

Self-destructive behaviour in general

Freud pointed out that there is a persistent conflict between the will to live and the will to die. Growth and the acceptance of responsibility are often painful and create trouble. Escape from the burdens of responsibility is an ever-present temptation. In most instances the devices of escape from life are partial. Usually the self-destructive quality of the escapes does not become clear to the person because most of the emotional satisfaction involved would be lost if he were obliged to face the meaning of his behaviour. His relief would be cancelled by feelings of guilt, and the behaviour would then serve no useful purpose.

In *Man Against Himself*, Menninger outlines the variety of techniques from the mild to the severe that man employs in self-destructive behaviour. He speaks of illness as a 'flight from frustration and the responsibilities of life', in short, a form of organic suicide.

Generally, it is difficult to recognize self-destructive behaviour from the external manifestations. This may be shown by such a simple matter as sleep. In the face of stress some persons retreat into sleep to escape responsibility, while others may actually need extra sleep in order to face their responsibilities effectively. The nature of the personality and the emotional roots of the behaviour determine its meaning.

Dr Flanders Dunbar points out that it is frustrating to the physician to treat a person who resists getting well. Deliberate efforts may be employed to avoid the treatments, while at the same time the person is acting as though he wants to get well. It may be as simple a matter as not taking one's medicine, or as complicated as a deep and resistant attitude towards the whole process involved in applying the healing arts.

It is pointed out by some doctors that a patient may begin to recover because he is tired of being ill, just as he became ill

because he was tired of facing the routine of responsibility of life. But no matter how the behaviour is judged, the fact remains that certain types of behaviour are self-destructive, whether applied a little at a time or in large doses. This may even be true of accidents and, in war, of self-inflicted wounds. Here a smaller and controlled injury is accepted in lieu of what might be a larger and uncontrolled injury. The retreat into illness involves more than we generally accept.

Physical aspects of self-destructive behaviour

The physical manifestations of illness vary according to the emotional nature and needs of the individual. It may well be that the emotional needs seek out a physical weakness, or even that habit prevails. Persons may persistently choose the same escapes from life. Also, it may be that we have a taste or a preference for certain types of illness and tend to move in that direction when emotional needs become acute.

Dunbar says that style is also a factor in the choice of disease, although it is an unconscious choice, to be sure. There is a tendency to acquire a disease that is fashionable or at least respectable.

Emotional contagion may also be a factor. An editor of one of the papers in a newspaper chain died suddenly of a heart attack. Within a few days three other editors in the group suffered heart attacks. The possibility of coincidence would have to be ruled out on mathematical grounds. Rather, it seems that the focusing of attention on the condition and the strenuous work that brought it on so stimulated the emotions of the men involved that they manifested the behaviour that is medically identified as heart disease.

This type of self-destructive behaviour may also be an expression of the will to live, and may involve escape for reasons of self-preservation. The soldier who accidentally shoots himself in the leg is sent to the hospital rather than the battlefield, and thus may prolong his life. The editor going to the hospital for a

long rest may be engaged in essentially the same type of
behaviour, although he may be less conscious of it.

Mr L was taken to a tuberculosis sanatorium. When he was
called on by his pastor he said, 'I was getting awfully tired. The
stress was building up and I could feel this thing coming on, but
there wasn't anything I could do. I'm just the type that can't
give up. This same thing happened to me about twelve years
ago when I had serious business trouble.' A type of unconscious
behaviour impelled him to take a long rest before something
more serious happened.

Perhaps it was someone like Mr L that Dr Dunbar had in
mind when she wrote,

> The mind which selects an illness is not at all related to that
> fortunately rare state of emotional upheaval which leads the
> victim to mutilate himself. The chooser of symptoms does
> not set out to get sick with malice aforethought. There must
> be a real emotional need for illness first. Then on the
> borderline between the known and the forgotten, the choice
> of symptoms is made.

In our culture, as long as illness is the accepted and respectable way for dealing with intolerable stress, we will have the
mildly destructive type of behaviour that destroys a little of life
in order to protect the whole of it.

The emotional roots of ill-health

Medical practice increasingly relates certain types of mental
and emotional condition to groups of physical symptoms called
a syndrome. Persistent anger and frustration is apt to lead to a
stomach ulcer, while fear and anxiety may be the forerunners of
heart disease. Persistent irritation tends toward dermatitis, and
unresolved grief to ulcerative colitis. So the understanding
grows of the relation of emotion to bodily states.

It is important to understand that there are physical condi-
tons not caused, as far as we know, by emotional or psychogenic
factors. For instance, a flyer shot down over the desert without

water will soon begin to suffer the effects of dehydration with all of the physical symptoms related to it. He is seriously ill, but the causative factor is simply absence of water in the system. A gourmet eats a poison toadstool with his mushrooms and soon his system is reacting to the unacceptable element that has been ingested. He is seriously ill, but no mental or emotional factor is related to the onset of the physical condition. However, the emotions very quickly become involved, and fear and anxiety are important factors determining the rate of his recovery. Although all disease has emotional ramifications, not all physical conditions are psychogenic in origin.

This moves us to a stage in considering man's total health where he is not concerned so much with symptoms or the scientific assault on the symptoms as with their deeper meaning. This is the prelude to the concept of wholeness of being that can achieve health at its highest possible level. Here the various branches of the healing arts are not in conflict, but can work together in mutual appreciation and shared understanding.

Speaking of the development of man's ability to deal with his own nature, Gerald Heard writes,

> The first great stage of advance was the physical, the second was the technical, the third must be the psychical. The first was unconscious, blind; the second is conscious, unreflective, aware of its need but not of itself, of how, not why; the third is inter-conscious, reflective, knowing not merely how to satisfy its needs but what they mean and what the whole means.[3]

For a long time illness was physical, a condition to be endured, for there was little that could be done. Then it was a contest for technical mastery over symptoms by those agents, chemical or surgical, that could be effectively employed. Now the emotional roots of ill-health are being laid bare by medical research itself, and we are approaching a new understanding of the nature of man and his needs as a physical and spiritual being.

Religion has something to say about the meaning of man and

life, and of the achievement of wholeness and health in man. But interestingly enough, science is also saying it clearly and well, with a respect for old values and now courage in facing their meaning. Let us look first at what science is saying.

6

Medically Defined Faith as an
Ingredient of Health

In Chapter 2 we examined a medically defined concept of faith
as basic to health, and in subsequent chapters we have tried to
expand our idea of the relation of mental and emotional states
to physical conditions of illness and health. In our effort to carry
this exploration further we will look at cases of specific persons
to see what the emotional state looked like as it lived and moved
among us.

In our exploration we will be dealing with much the same
phenomena as religion employs in working with people, except
that our sources and evaluations will be in the medical context.

Examining the nature of faith

The basic premise of psychosomatic research is that cause-effect
factors are at work in producing the malfunction of organs. If
the effect or the symptoms can be properly observed, in a broad
enough context, it may be possible to discover the cause. If only
the symptoms are treated, there may be superficial response
through symptom removal or symptom displacement, but the
causative factor may remain. If, however, the cause is properly
perceived, then treatment may be more adequate, for then the
medical intervention may deal more directly with the real cause
rather than the mere symptoms.

Similarly, the research in psychosomatics may be able to
throw light on the causative forces that are at work to restore or

maintain health. If faith can be a contributor to healing, it can also be active in preventing physical breakdown and organic malfunction.

William James, a philosopher, psychologist and professor of medicine at Harvard Medical School, described a ladder of faith by which one could climb step by step to a state of firm conviction. It was related to his concept that a person could significantly manage the course of his organic behaviour by his 'will to believe'. The steps up this ladder of faith were:

There is nothing absurd in a certain view of the world being true, nothing contradictory.
It might have been true under certain conditions.
It may be true even now.
It is fit to be true.
It ought to be true.
It shall be true for me.

Probably more than we realize, each of us employs a system of our own which approximates these steps of faith, or their equally significant negative counterparts, the steps of doubt. The opposite of faith seems to be fear or anxiety. The hypochondriac appears to use the steps in an order that moves from apprehension to a fulfilment of the fear in the acting-out of the anxiety organically.

Even the most firmly fixed scientific minds seem to give way to speculation and personal prejudices when they face points where their scientific system does not function. For instance, Einstein says that 'the supreme task of the physicist is the discovery of the most elemental general laws from which the world picture can be deduced logically', but he admits that this goal can never be achieved, for the mind is inadequate to the task. However, this does not prevent him from knowing with assurance that his hypotheses are valid. His knowing, then, is more an act of faith than it is an act of reason.

Similarly, Max Planck is sure of the predetermined course of events logically, but it is not because he has been able to prove his assumptions but rather because he is 'convinced' of their

validity. Conviction is a form of emotion, and here his conviction is not supported by his scientific observation, though it may not offend it.

Much the same sort of reasoning is active in the individual in relation to his health, and in the medical profession in relation to its conviction concerning the value of its method and its philosophical assumptions.

Faith is made up of three ingredients: at the mental level its beliefs, at the emotional level its convictions, and at the physical level in its processes of acting out organically. All three may be active and in differing proportions when one assesses the impact of someone's faith on his health or illness.

Unconscious factors in faith

Powerful unconscious forces at work in the life of an individual may veto his rational perceptions. Often the physical symptoms observed are rooted in the lower levels of consciousness and are the acting out of this powerful though inaccessible part of the being.

This may be encountered in medical practice where sensory organs are involved. Certain types of blindness may be rooted in an unwillingness to see. Certain types of deafness may develop from a desire to avoid hearing something unpleasant. Often in these cases the syndrome is classified as hysterical behaviour, which is an easy way of avoiding the deeper levels of consciousness that may be responsible. As one physician reports, he told a blind patient that in order to see 'he must not only open his eyes but he must also use his brains and look'. The patient failed to respond to this suggestion, so the physician then approached him through a lower level of consciousness. 'The following day his condition was unchanged, and I decided to try some psychotherapy on him. He was very easily placed in a hypnotic state and then told that at the count of ten he would be able to see. At the count of ten he did not fail me, and has enjoyed normal vision since that moment.' But then, interestingly, the physician continues with this judgment. 'This form of

therapy which fills the entire bag of tricks of the Christian Scientist and chiropractor and other cultists, might well be put to more frequent use by ourselves, and would be if we recognized more often the psychogenic nature of many conditions.'

What the physician was saying, in effect, was that more attention to the unconscious roots of organic malfunction might prove effective. But by indirection he was saying that certain forms of non-medical healing were able to produce healing because they were more attentive to the whole person and his needs than they were to superficial symptoms.

In a compensation case another physician reports similar results through environmental change. 'Dr Hammes followed up every form of suggestive therapy at his command. We were unable to obtain any improvement in his case, and he was finally discharged with the recommendation that he be compensated for total loss of vision. However, about this time, his family troubles reached a crisis and his vision returned. He returned to work and completely dropped his claim for compensation.' Obviously, something in his family life caused the blindness and a change in his family life restored his vision. The subtle states of personal and environmental influence may so profoundly affect the unconscious condition of an individual that it changes his function. If the blind man who sought compensation had been told that it was his family condition that was so influencing his unconscious defences that it was making him blind, he would have had difficulty believing it. But all of the evidence was provided to prove that point when the conditions changed enough to relieve the deep inner protective device he used to produce his non-seeing state.

So apprehensive are some physicians, that they even apologize to their colleagues for successful treatment. In a case where suggestion was the primary source of therapeutic intervention, Dr J. B. Horgan says, 'In as much as this case leans rather on the dramatic than the scientific, I feel I owe the members an apology for bringing it forward at a meeting like this. I feel also that, though successful, the treatment adopted was neither orthodox nor scientific.' Recently a psychiatrist in

California told me that he used exorcism in treating certain persons with disturbed emotional states with immediate success. However, he added, 'You can bet I would never report that to the county medical association.'

The admission from these practitioners of modern medicine is quite clearly that methods do not have to be orthodox to be successful. It is further implied that in dealing with the subconscious it may well be that the orthodox is inappropriate, and may need to be re-examined before too many patients have to suffer from a form of prejudice that could be unwarranted.

The faith that works through the unconscious may be beyond reasoned approaches, both in the effect it has of producing disease and the significance it might have in providing a restoration of healthful function.

Conscious processes in faith

At the conscious level of response a person may most easily indicate his disposition by the way he handles pain. Pain is an indicator of malfunction in many instances, though not all. Pain is often a sign of vigour and active resistance on the part of the organism. But like inflammation, there can be an over-reaction which tends to amplify the disturbance out of proportion. It is a part of the experience of most of us to know that little things may cause great discomfort, and some of the more serious disturbances have little sensation of pain. A toothache or an earache can disorganize life, while a broken back or a broken pelvis may produce no comparable sensation.

What the conscious mind does with these sensations may amplify or reduce the pain. The way a person thinks and feels about his illness may prolong it or hasten the healing process. Numerous researches are providing evidence that the duration of illness among persons is associated with psychological indicants, that the more favourable the incidents with respect to the mental health of the individual, the shorter the duration of the illness. There is evidence also that the psychological condition of patients is a good prognosticator of the effectiveness of

medical treatment. The incidence of somatic disease among persons with definite psychological disturbance is substantially greater than normally expected, and a relationship between psychological disorder and various forms of sociocultural separation and disintegration has been indicated in a large number of studies. People who use their minds to create problems are effective in doing just that. Worriers give themselves something to worry about.

In a study of persons done with the Minnesota Multiphasic Personality Inventory it was found that those who showed a depressive state before the onset of an attack of Asian flu had symptoms fifty per cent longer than those who were largely free of depression. Just as some people are accident prone, so others have the mental attitude that makes them illness prone. As they can direct their conscious mind to think of the things they choose to dwell on, they may use their minds to make themselves ill.

In some studies to explore the way people experience pain and discomfort, it was determined that there are two basic types of people, those who tend to reduce their awareness of discomfort and those who augment their pain by their mental attitude toward it. In efforts to discover what happens when aspirin is ingested, the response of the augmentors was measured. To the best of the knowledge of the researchers, the effect of the aspirin was to make the augmentors temporarily into reducers. This may not always be helpful to a person, for at times the pain is a danger signal, but when people are always complaining, it may be that they are seeking means of escape from painful life experience and so incorporate it in bodily behaviour. In a study of sick and healthy people it was found that few of the healthy ones had serious life problems which those who were chronically ill or sickness-prone had during their adult lives, divorces, separations, conflict with parents, siblings, husbands and wives, uncongenial living and working conditions. In other words, they were the ones who had developed little skill in managing crises, and so incorporated them into their total response to life.

They were sicker when they were sick because they were actually sicker when they were not sick.

It is clearly possible for people to develop a clear and conscious perspective on their living. Often this is the goal of a counselling process. The person may learn to understand why he directs his energy towards pain and illness, and then he can learn just as well to use his conscious mind to avoid the pitfalls of this type of conscious conspiracy against himself and his health.

Super-conscious expressions of faith

The dimension of mental activity that is employed by the Yogi, the level of mental achievement that is defined by Sorokin and the students of genius, as well as the mental perspective of the person who might be called the superhealthy person in Maslow's terms, needs to be looked at to discover how this upper level of consciousness can be employed in producing healing and in maintaining health.

In her book, *Breakthrough to Creativity*, Dr Karagulla asks, 'Is Higher Sense Perception a kind of superconscious activity which may ultimately prove to be a next step in man's evolutionary development?' And she answers, 'Man must become aware of his superconscious and able to tap this creative level of full awareness.' The possibilities for the use of this higher sensitivity can have medical, individual and social benefits.

Dr Karagulla sees energy at work in various forms of healing processes. She finds that people with the heightened sensitivity can perceive energy force-fields in things as well as people. For instance, these persons can feel a magnet and know which is the negative and the positive end by the way they experience warmth and coolness. This special sensitivity seems to appear among the more healthful and intelligent individuals, though at this point it is not easily determined which is the cause and which is the effect.

Dr George S. White, an American physician, became aware of a field of energy surrounding each person and he observed

changes in this energy field that gave clues to illness and health in the individual. Eventually he was able to identify certain types of changes in the auric field as being related to certain diseases. He has used these perceptions of the force field diagnostically as explained in his book, *The Story of the Human Aura* (1928).[1]

This super-conscious capacity sometimes shows itself in forms of instant perception such as that achieved by Professor Aitken of Edinburgh University, whose mathematical ability seemed to be related to instant perception of vast fields of human knowledge in extrasensory ways.

The super-conscious state seems to make persons accessible to energy sources that can have beneficial effect on states of health.

> These energies move in and out of our individual fields in a similar fashion to the process of breathing. Each individual seems to have his own selective process for taking in various types of energy. Certain activities of stimuli key in or give access to this ocean of energy. Other activities or emotional states may decrease the access to surrounding energies. Grief or self-centredness, for example, appear greatly to diminish the individual's access to this energy supply.

This may well explain the high death rate among widows the first year after the death of a husband, or the higher percentage of hospital admissions among persons in acute grief.

This super-conscious sensitivity may show itself in heightened awareness of others and in communication with others. The phenomena appear to be basic to intercessory prayer where another person is held in loving concern and large numbers of coincidences occur. In the nineteenth century English government officials openly admitted that there were people in India who were able to transport messages telepathically the whole length or breadth of India in a matter of minutes. The person with higher sense perception appears to have a variety of paranormal resources at his disposal. So it seems that the super healthy person and the super-conscious ability and the para-

normal abilities come together to produce a special type of skill that may be a goal for man's spiritual development.

All there is of a person is involved in the way he meets life. His faith in life has many components, but they can be used positively to move him in the direction of a superhealthy state of being. He has responsibility for the way his varied abilities may be used. He can discipline and refine his skills, or he can neglect them. The nature of his faith is inseparably bound up with the way he uses the resources of life for good or ill.

7

The Anatomy of Faith

Functioning in inner space

Man has pushed the frontiers of his explorations right off the face of the earth, and journeys to the moon and probes to other heavenly bodies have become routine. Yet one of the first of the astronauts to set foot on the moon has returned to earth with a desire to explore man, the inner space that is so important to his living. As if this were the important direction of research in the years ahead, Dr Edgar Mitchell has set up a research foundation scientifically to explore the unusual abilities of man himself. Some of these abilities have been taken for granted and others have been ignored because they did not fit any of the usual modes of scientific examination.

A whole generation of young people disillusioned by the philosophy of production and consumption as the measurement of life's meaning have been exploring the dimensions of consciousness. Sometimes this exploration has been headlong and dangerous, with the use of chemical agents that were little understood. At other times it was a quest for disciplines that could illuminate the capacity for sensation and response in the depths of consciousness. Recently in the college where I taught I suggested introducing a course on the history of man's concepts of his consciousness. The course was listed as 'Theories of Consciousness'. To the surprise of all concerned this course proved to be the most popular elective course on the campus

that term. Youth show an active interest in their inner being, what it means and how it functions to enrich or limit life.

Certainly if this interest in inner space can be used creatively it could have a bearing on the way health is perceived and managed by a whole generation of those who are now becoming adults. This would have a bearing on diet, the movement away from highly refined foods and the additives that are unnecessary limits of nutrition. For while the person may not be merely what he eats, it is equally true that what he ingests may have a bearing on his energy, his attitudes and his general health.

Reductionism versus enhancing life

Two basic philosophical systems are at work among those who explore health. One seeks to reduce the examined phenomena into a small system of thought. Of course, the benefits of this reduction are obvious, for then it can all be kept in a safe, manageable and limited framework. This makes the limiting philosopher feel more secure, for then he is in control. If anything does not fit his little system, he can try to ignore it or deny its validity. He can claim it is not worthy of consideration or is actually a mere happenstance that shows how it takes an exception to prove a rule.

In medical practice the limiting philosophy has often been employed because it makes it easier for the physician to function within the realm of the comfortable and the known. When man is reduced to chemical interaction or mechanical interrelation, a whole lot of other disturbing phenomena can be discounted as irrelevant.

A second viewpoint tries to make room not only for the familiar but for the unfamiliar, not only for those things that fit the rules, but also for those exceptions that do not prove rules but may indicate that there are some other rules that may be at work. The researchers in the paranormal processes observed in healing have come to look upon man as more highly endowed and more amazing than had even been assumed. Here the old frames of reference may be fractured, but room may be made

for new discoveries. These discoveries include not only phenomena having to do with meditation and prayer for healing, but the use of such ancient practices as the laying on of hands and even the investigation of more spectacular healing processes such as Alexis Carrel observed at Lourdes and Henry Puharik witnessed in Brazil with a psychic healer named Arigo.

Dr Puharik, who has done research in aerospace medicine, and was senior research scientist for New York University Medical Center, organized a team of scientists to go to Brazil and check out on the spot a person named Arigo who had quite a local reputation for bizarre and unorthodox medical practice. Mr Arigo had a most limited education and worked in the local post office. But each day dozens of people came to him for healing, and he treated them with amazing success. Often he would write prescriptions, and sometimes he would employ crude surgery with no anaesthetic or precautions against infection. Figuring that there must be something going on here that should be brought under careful medical scrutiny, Dr Puharik and his team set up a tent with the latest portable medical diagnostic equipment. As patients came in the early morning before Mr Arigo went to work, they would examine them before they went in for his treatment and after they came out. They checked the prescriptions and found them to be almost without exception what they would have prescribed. They checked the surgery and found no sign of infection then or later, and in each instance the patient presented a wound that appeared to be about six months old as far as the healing process was concerned. Instead of his being rejected by the local medical profession, a special wing was being built on the hospital to accommodate him and his patients. At no point was any valid explanation given for the unusual phenomena observed, but the evidence spoke for itself. When interviewed, Mr Arigo explained that he was possessed by the spirit of a deceased physician who was responsible for all that was done. In view of the phenomena observed it may seem as good an explanation as any. Dr Puharik had minor surgery on his arm and described his feeling as being like a quick passing of an icicle over his skin. The scar appeared

to be not only healed but months old in the instant after the surgery was performed. While there appears to be no valid medical explanation for things like this, there is a growing body of carefully documented medical evidence that these things occur under careful medical scrutiny.

The reductionists' approach to these phenomena might be to deny their validity or ignore them as far as possible. The enhancer would explore all possible theories with the sure knowledge that where there is an effect, there must also be an adequate cause if he can find it.

The energy that can transform living

In various ways we have assumed that faith is a form of life-actualizing energy. When faith is at work to change a person from an enhancer to a reducer, things become obviously different in his organic behaviour. The power of faith produces measurable change in the ways a person performs. It marks the difference between a depressive response to life and a fulfilled form of living.

But actually we have done little study of faith apart from its religious manifestations. We need to go deeper.

Anatomy is the study of organic function that is below the surface. It cannot be seen by a superficial glance, but rather calls for dissection and depth exploration.

The usual study of faith tends to proceed along superficial lines, with an examination of those aspects of faith that are consciously held. For our purposes we will approach faith in depth, dissecting the consciousness, and seeking to understand the larger dimensions of faith.

This study in depth has not been possible until our own period in history, for although there have been strong indications of mental life extended beyond the boundaries of consciousness, there has been no ordered knowledge about these areas of mental activity below and above consciousness until modern psychiatric and psychoanalytic study accumu-

lated a body of experience and clinical observation that verified the theories posited by men like Myers and Freud.

For our purposes we will define faith as the power of cosmic energy at work in man. This faith permeates all of life like yeast in bread or like the Pauli principle at work in the nature of matter. It is a force that cannot be seen or measured by any known method of measuring, but the effects of it are as clearly evident as the light of the sun is evident as a force in the growth of plant life.

It is a complicated force and difficult to analyse. For we may feel that our faith is developed by the things we say to ourselves consciously, but often the things that we say to ourselves consciously are motivated by feelings that are deeply rooted in unconscious areas of our mind's life. Similarly we may be moved by intuition, revelation, or the impact of telepathic communication in a way that modifies our conscious and unconscious mental processes. The importance of this is to force us to be more completely aware than ever before that man is an indivisible unity, and he cannot be dealt with in any other way. Any analysis of the parts must always be aware of the whole, and any approach to the whole must be aware of the multiplicity of the parts.

It is also important to realize that faith is highly personal, individualistic, and therefore varied in its expressions. No one can live on the faith of another. The only faith an individual can ever have is his own. It must be individually released and developed. Others can inspire it, guide its growth, enrich it, but the individual integrates it and makes it real for himself. This power of faith is a way of being in the universe.

Faith deals with a real power, and therefore it must be bound up with reality. Some healing cults are illusion-creating and give the full force of their mind and emotion to denying reality. They say illness is not real and therefore it does not exist. The faith we are dealing with opposes the creation of illusion, and gives itself fully to a stern facing of reality, but it does this in the name of the greatest of all realities. It recognizes the reality of illness, and it cooperates with all methods of restoring health,

but it does it in the name of a faith, a spiritual force, a healing reality that is a more powerful force than the drives toward illness.

In doing this it knows that all power exists and no power is created. The existing power is channelled, transformed and used, but it is not made. The engineers who developed the power resources of Niagara Falls employed their intelligence and their skills in using the materials to take the power that already existed in nature and gave it a new direction so that it could be transformed into the kind of power that would light lights, run motors and enrich the standard of living of people for miles around. None of the engineers thought he was making energy. He was engaged in transforming it for purposes he conceived. He was using and developing power rather than ignoring it.

In speaking of faith as the power of the cosmos at work in man, we are doing the same thing. We are not creating any power that is not already there potentially. But we are trying to develop the kind of understanding, the kind of intelligence, the kinds of skills in the use of it, that will make it possible to transform the power into a life-creating, life-fulfilling reality. The main items of the electrical engineers' trade are the transformers which adapt the existent power to the needs of the consumer of power. In this respect faith is the power, and the disciplined spiritual energy of the individual would be the transformer which adapts the power to individual needs.

J. A. Hadfield, the London psychiatrist, writes of the psychology of power as if it were the expression of the instinct of self-assertion, 'Confidence, deriving its power from the instinct of self-assertion, turns weakness into strength and failure into success.'

In amplifying the processes by which this power is engaged, Hadfield speaks of the power of the unconscious to affect life.

In the hypnotic experiment on fatigue the subject could only grip twenty-nine pounds, because he said, 'I am weak, I cannot grip it any harder.' When he said, and believed, 'I am

strong and powerful', his strength was multiplied fivefold. I suddenly told another man that he could not talk; he tried, but found that he was dumb – simply because, being suggestible to my words, he lost confidence in his power to speak, and believed what I suggested to be in fact true. In all such cases we have seen that the will alone does not ensure success. 'To will is present with me, but how to perform I know not.' That which is lacking is 'confidence'. I have spoken of the paralysing effects of fear. Confidence removes this paralysis and turns belief into a mighty impulse to act. It fills men with the strength which makes the soul master of its fate. It possesses the timid who cling to the shores of life, who have toiled all night and caught nothing, and bids them launch out into the deep, where endeavour is crowned with overwhelming success. Want of belief in its possibility is always the main obstacle to the performing of any mighty work. Faith in its possibility – a faith not necessarily founded on evidence but one that dares to take the risk – is the greatest asset to success in any task. 'If thou canst?' 'All things are possible to them that believe.'

So a psychiatrist describes the power of faith at work in human life. But the definition of the power as a function of emotional economy does not explain the source of the power adequately. To use Hadfield's own words:

Nature is economic in her gifts: she will not give strength to those who will not expend it. These remain uninspiring and uninspired. She is lavish in her gifts to those who will use them, and especially to those who devote them to nature's altruistic ends, for such ends harmonize the soul. Life demands expression. If the life-stream that flows through us finds the channel blocked by a life of inactivity, we inevitably suffer from staleness and boredom, or a sense of physical debility. A purposeless life is a life of fatigue. . . It is a law of nature – a law of life – that only by giving shall we receive. None is so healthy and fresh as he who gives freely of his strength, and thereby liberates his impulses and instinctive

powers into quickened activity. This is of immense practical importance. In the treatment of neurasthenia, the chief symptom of which is fatigue, it is often found that the 'Weir Mitchell' treatment of inactivity and isolation is the worst a physician can prescribe. Already is the patient suffering from too much self-consciousness and introspection. Some disappointment or sorrow may have taken all the life out of him. . . Give such a man 'something to live for', that awakens his interest, and his ambition will arouse his instinctive emotions till the heart that was sluggish palpitates with the joy of life once more, and nerves tingle with eager expectation. Life's demand for expression will be satisfied.[1]

What Hadfield is saying is that the normal, healthy life is its own transformer, and that the life of purpose gives direction to the instinctive emotions so that power is released and the being is charged with the energy that is nature's gift to those who are willing to use it.

Perhaps it is just at this point that our examination of the power released by faith must be explored deeply. For the same power that releases the energy for creative work is the power that restores an ill body to wholeness. The nature of the power is considerable, but our knowledge of the laws for its use, and the methods for its understanding, are incomplete.

Santayana gives some clues in his study of *Scepticism and Animal Faith*, for the animal is more completely given to the direction of his instinctual emotions, and less subject to self-conscious thought, with its life-modifying effects. The self-consciousness with its burdens and its privileges may well either inhibit or stimulate the employment of nature's resources for healthful and effective living.

It may be at just this point that we are led to the re-examination of what faith is and what it does. Our efforts at understanding will be functional and not philosophical, although the philosophy will certainly be implicit.

To restate the problem simply, we are dealing with a force, and a life-changing force. But the power of the force is in man,

not because he made it but because he is so made. However, his power of thought, his self-consciousness, and his capacity for choice may be limited to pervert this power. On the other hand, with proper direction he may transform the power into life-giving energy and productivity. It becomes the source of his true wholeness of being.

The rational perception of life-actualizing forces

The energy of life need not be a frightening mystery. It can be rationally perceived and creatively used to move human potential toward an achieved actual. Maslow's view of 'full humanness' seeks to move beyond a limited view of man so that the possibilities latent in each person can be released for the enjoyment of life and health.

Maslow speaks of the Jonah complex. This is the attitude towards consciousness that makes it a burden rather than a privilege. The person who harbours deep fears concerning his inadequacy constantly seeks to be thrown overboard to relieve the ship of its jinx. The ways he employs to do this are constantly to discount his value to himself and others. In this way he uses his endowment of consciousness to destroy his capacity rather than realize the full benefits of it. He tends to deny his own uniqueness and claim that there is only one unique being in creation and that is his deity. The God becomes the scapegoat to relieve him of responsibility for becoming the person he might be because he would not want to develop his own uniqueness: that might be sacrilege.

In his physical manifestations, it might show up as impotence or frigidity, as the acting out of a fear of one's own power for love and expression. With illness it might follow a similar course, for a person would choose to be ill rather than face the implications of his health for life. Health as an obligation to life would become an excuse for retreat from life. So the potential to become a superhealthy person would be lost in the fear that the consciousness of obligation for health would lay on life.

Maslow outlines the attitudes and steps that may be taken to

move beyond perverted consciousness that results in personal impotence and illness. These forms of behaviour can be followed by a person who wants to set creative directions for his living within rational and attainable bounds.

Self-actualization means experiencing fully, vividly, self-lessly, with full concentration and total absorption. This means the encountering of life and all that is a part of it without adolescent self-consciousness and with an adult freedom to be one's best self without apology or hostile self-judgment.

When a person moves through life, he encounters an endless series of choices. The future is built on each of these decisions. He can regress or he can move ahead at each point. The creative person does not have to pay tribute to his unnecessary defences by retreating before life, but he can use each choice as an opportunity to grow and become more fully the person he was intended to be.

A creative person can learn to listen to his spontaneous impulses, for they may well be the point where he encounters life free of his defences against growth. If he acts on his healthy impulses he can move ahead into life, whereas if he waits and ponders he may give his immature and unhealthy defences a chance to catch up with him.

This calls for a type of honesty that may be hard to develop. The person who is afraid of life is apt to be constantly lying to himself, deceiving himself and frustrating himself by his false self-image. Perhaps the most difficult task in growth is to be completely honest with yourself. And if a person cannot be honest with himself, there is little chance that he can be truly honest with anyone else. This is where game-playing comes in, for the games we play with ourselves and others are apt to be the thinly disguised forms of deceit we develop to avoid life and its opportunities for growth.

This leads to a satisfaction in experience of your own best response to life. The actualized self becomes the point where a respect for one's thought and feelings are made evident. Then you do not have to trust the critics to decide whether or not you like a play, and read the book reviews to decide whether or not

you can enjoy a book. The self emerges as mature and willing to trust fully its own validity.

Then the self-actualizing behaviour becomes part of a process of building a more adequate person. Each choice helps to make the next one more authentic, and the valid self grows in creative skills as well as in self-confidence. The inner being then becomes the measure of life rather than a shallow echo of external forces.

When these growth skills are developed, the peak-experiences of life may tend to become normative rather than fleeting moments of self-realization. The joy of living can then become an increasing experience and the fear and anxiety will be eliminated.

Too often people seek excuses for failure or for illness. They blame parents, or circumstances, or the inadequacy of their own being. None of this effort to blame others adds anything of value to life. It merely confirms the variety of escapes from responsibility that can be developed by imaginative persons who pervert their capacity for consciousness.

The superhealthy person follows a clearly marked and completely rational course of healthy growth. He moves beyond the abuse of his creativity to his wise use of this powerful resource. Just as his faith can be directed toward low and self-destructive ends, and produce illness, so this self-verifying inner resource can be used for his development into a more adequate and fulfilled being.

The choices are in his hands. He cannot fruitfully blame others for the way he uses his capacity for creativity. More than he may like to realize, his destiny is in his own keeping. Just as faith in medicine may help to overcome disease, so faith in the superhealthy endowment of each person may overcome tragic reductionism and self-fear.

Let us now move more deeply into our examination of the ways in which this creative faith may manifest itself in life, for this may well reveal not only the sources of illness but also the resources for becoming a superhealthy person.

8

Faith that is Innate

What we would speak of as an innate faith may be referred to by others as pattern, design or unconscious purpose.

It is essentially a capacity of response to life at whatever level it is lived.

In an ant it would be an instinctive pattern of social organization.

In an oyster it would be a capacity to turn irritating grains of sand into pearls.

In an oriole it would be an ability to build a hanging nest even if it had never seen one.

In a man it would be shown by the inner power that will heal a wound even when a patient is in a state of depression that turns his conscious mental processes against his own innate will to be whole.

The built-in pattern of faith

It is important to know what it is that the conscious mind is cooperating with at the lower levels of consciousness in order to know how the power of faith can be fully employed.

If a person cuts his finger, he immediately becomes an exhibit of the cooperation of conscious and unconscious forces for healing. The body with its innate wisdom goes to work to bring to the injured area its emergency treatment equipment. This goes to work to stop the flow of blood, and build a temporary skin that we call a scab. Having done this first important piece

of work, the body then marshals its resources for a more leisurely and more highly specialized repair job with the building of the scar tissue and the pushing away of the scab. In these tasks blood cells that are equipped for their tasks are brought to the area with a pattern and design that shows purposeful activity. It is intelligent response, though it is surely not conscious response, for the same process can take place if the person is unconscious. At first the scar tissue is red and obvious, but with the passing of time it is so modified that it is difficult to recognize which is the area that was cut from the rest of the surrounding skin tissue.

This healing process is so basic, so fundamental to life that it is interfered with only with difficulty. Surgeons testify that the attitude of mind of a patient has an effect upon the healing process, so they do not like to operate upon a person in a depressed state of mind. However, though a depressed person, looking at his cut finger and lamenting the fact that it will never heal, may slow up the process, the innate built-in wisdom of his body is stronger than the self-destructive thoughts that may possess him. Though he may interfere with the healing process it is not likely that at that point at least he will completely stop it.

It is a psychological truism that thought persistently directed to any part of the body will increase the flow of blood to that area. This can be effectively demonstrated under hypnosis when the subconscious mind is brought into direct activity through the agency of another conscious mind that is directing it.

But the interesting thing is that there are instances of regeneration and healing of tissue through this kind of a thought-process which is not deliberate, but which in some way seems to trigger the basic response of the body towards its own wholeness.

An interesting illustration of this was observed by the author. A parishioner came to his pastor and said with some embarrassment that he knew prayer was for important things, but that he had an injured toe on his right foot. Because it was the large toe, it interfered with his work, caused considerable

discomfort, and had not responded to a variety of treatments that had been applied to it. The parishioner wondered if the pastor thought it would be too trivial a matter to pray about. The pastor assured him that if it was important enough for him to make the request, it was certainly important enough to be a subject of the specialized kind of thinking that prayer is. After explaining just what was involved, there was a brief prayer, and the parishioner was assured that his name would be added to the prayer list of one of the prayer groups in the parish for continued consideration. It had been emphasized that prayer was not necessarily directed toward an injured part as much as towards the health and wholeness of the entire being.

The interesting part of the matter is that the pastor had injured his large toe on his right foot fifteen years before when he had dropped a three hundred pound reel of cable on it. The toenail had been mashed, but no bone was broken, and no special treatment was given it apart from treading lightly for a few days. When the injury healed, the toenail was deformed, badly twisted, and more than a quarter of an inch thick on one side. Nothing was done about it, and no thought was given to it during fifteen intervening years. It was accepted as one of the minor deformities that are a part of the body's adjustment to injury. The condition had remained unchanged during fifteen years.

The night after praying for the parishioner and his injury, the pastor's large toe on his right foot began to ache. It throbbed and ached for nearly three months. At the end of three months there was a completely new and normal toenail on that foot, and it has remained so now for several years. Some sensitive mechanism of being seems to have been set in motion to restore an injured area to wholeness. For some unknown reason the restorative process had been held in abeyance for fifteen years. It appears that some unconscious thought-process directed the flow of blood towards that area with enough of a concentration to start in motion the normal regenerative forces that are a part of the body's natural wisdom.

An interesting sidelight on this process is that there was no

change in the condition of the toe of the parishioner, and after a period of time a surgical operation was recommended by the physician in question as the only way he could think of for resolving the difficulty.

Any increase in our understanding of the factors affecting health that are beyond the level of consciousness is important for our understanding of the total problem. For this reason it is useful to examine the spectrum of consciousness as Dr Frederick W. F. Myers describes it in the opening chapters of his book, *Human Personality*.

Dr Myers likens the spectrum of consciousness to the spectrum of light. Our eyes are conscious only of the white light which can be broken up into the colours of the rainbow. These are all visible to the human eye. These are the colours that the mind through the agency of the eye is conscious of. However, light radiation extends beyond both ends of the visible spectrum. The mind can be made aware of them indirectly, but there is no direct consciousness. On the slow-moving side of the spectrum there are the types of heat radiation with infra-red and slower moving rays of light. These are important for life, and our bodies are sensitive to them even though our eyes are not. To that extent they are beyond the range of visual consciousness. At the other end of the spectrum are the fast-moving forms of light radiation such as the ultra-violet, gamma, x-ray and cosmic radiation. These, too, are important for our living, and life could not long be sustained without their beneficial effects, but we are never visually conscious of such light without the aid of special devices that supplement our vision. But when someone looks at a photographic plate that has been exposed to high speed radiation, he can see how porous he is and become aware of yet another aspect of his own being, well beyond that which is revealed to him through his visual equipment.

So each of our senses works within a range of stimuli to which it is conscious, but these stimuli do not represent the full range of that which exists.

So it is with the levels or spectrum of consciousness. There is that of which we are consciously aware and which is subject to

the process of thinking, recollection and reasoning. This would include the areas of faith that would deal with belief and reason, extending below the level of consciousness, or in more general usage, the subconscious, the preconscious or the unconscious. Comparable to the slow-moving rays of light, they are continually affecting our lives, though we may not be aware of them. They can be brought to consciousness by special methods such as dreams, hypnosis, or free association. At the other side of the spectrum of consciousness are the equivalent of the fast-moving rays of light, what Myers called the super-liminal or the super-conscious. This, too, may be profoundly affecting our living, though we may be equally unaware of it. We can gain insight into its nature through special avenues of sensitivity which make it possible for us to see through ourselves as it were with new understanding. Visions, telepathic sensitivity, what we have traditionally called the indwelling of the Holy Spirit, are some of the ways by which our consciousness is extended into the super-conscious.

But all consciousness is one, just as all being is a living unit. We do not understand all the ways by which the interrelations of being are at work, but we are continually learning that which pushes our frontiers of understanding back a bit further. Perhaps Freud was close to an important insight when he said that he equated consciousness with electricity. If only we knew what electricity was!

All these levels of consciousness work upon each other in those matters that affect and reveal the nature of faith.

Adaptation to things

We would be inclined to think that the adaptations of beings to inanimate things would be largely a conscious process plus that conditioned consciousness which for convenience sake is pressed below the level of ordered thought and called habit. But here the consciousness seems to work at all three levels.

Parents presented their three-year-old son for baptism. He had no verbal competence and would not be able consciously to

recall the event five years later, but as the parents approached the pastor the youngster began a loud protest. The parents explained the situation in this way. 'He thinks you are a doctor and that you are going to stick him with a needle.' A highly developed form of thing-consciousness was at work in the mind of this child to establish associations of pain and pleasure. It is reasonable to believe that he would wince for a long time at the sight of a hypodermic needle, or a person whom he took to be a bearer of such an item.

The process of growth with its varied experiences involves a great deal of thing-consciousness. The adaptation to the external world which a young child takes in easy stages as his sensory equipment develops, is a long and slow process. It is a process that never ends, but all of the emotions attached to the early stages of this development are stored in the lower levels of consciousness, and so can be at work to affect behaviour without being brought directly into the orbit of conscious reasoning or thinking processes.

Much of the growth process invites a trust or faith in things. The floor is solid and can be trusted to hold one's weight. The light switch can be trusted to bring light. An infinite and intricate fabric of things that can be trusted becomes a part of the innate equipment with which the lower level of consciousness is equipped for facing life.

It does not seem applicable to talk of a super-conscious factor involved in relation to things and adaptation to things. But even here there are evidences of influences that seem to invite this form of explanation. Dr Rhine's explorations with psychokinesis show direct influence of thought on inanimate objects, and although far from conclusive, are at least suggestive in that direction. Experiments in the modification of animate and inanimate objects as a result of intense high frequency radiation may throw light on this subject. Experiments already reported show that amoebae respond to radio waves. Experiments by the Air Force and Westinghouse dealing with the amplification of telepathic waves may produce interesting results at this point.

Adaptation to people

Thing-consciousness is merged with person-consciousness. A child merges his physical needs with the physical being of his mother so that in the early stages of life there is no definite line between where he ends and mother begins. This kind of a merging of person with group becomes the basis for the innate group-consciousness. Add to this the deeply ingrained herd instinct, and the force of the group consciousness becomes a factor of great importance. Some of the phenomena that appear to be healings stimulated by prayer may be explained by the activating of this kind of an awareness of group support that stimulates an important response as far as unconscious or innate group dependence is concerned. The person separated from the group and its support, even unconsciously, is emotionally sustained by the knowledge that a group of persons are bringing the resources of their minds and spirits together on his behalf. The type of support modifies consciousness at its lower levels with the change of physical condition that is interpreted as healing.

Here again, the relation of person-consciousness to the lower levels of emotional response is shown through the transference phenomena, where the physical being of one person is invested with the feelings that one has held towards another. In its technical sense this becomes an important aid in psychotherapy. In its non-technical form it is a common part of experience. We like someone instantaneously, even before we know anything about them, because some deep emotional association makes us feel a pleasurable response. Or we may dislike someone with no reasonable explanation. We say, 'I don't know why it is, but I just do not like that person.' This is the tag-line of the negative transference, where the subconscious association exerts its influence on person-consciousness, and in doing so modifies our behaviour in relation to people.

The conscious processes employed in dealing with people are continually being modified by intrusion from the spectrum of consciousness beyond the conscious. Perhaps more than we

realize, this is true of those impulses that come from the super-conscious. George Devereau's book on *Psychoanalysis and the Occult* leads us to believe that the processes of telepathic communication are far more common than we usually assume. One psychoanalyst says that all of his patients seem to have some capacity for it. This may explain how strong emotions like anxiety can be communicated so readily across great distances. It may also give a clue as to the therapeutic effects of intercessory prayer.

The super-conscious factor appears to be most actively at work between the minds of persons who for some reason have a strong emotional bond. In studies of spontaneous telepathic communication the number of cases involving those who were strangers or mere acquaintances was about twenty per cent of the total, with all the rest involving relatives or close friends.

So the processes of adaptation of person to person are continually employing all levels of consciousness, whether we are aware of it or not.

Adaptation of cosmic reality

Here adaptation begins with an innate capacity to take the beneficial radiation that comes from cosmic sources and turn it into the stuff of life. It is unconsciously done, and shares much the same quality as that of the flower which takes the light of the sun and through the processes of photosynthesis makes it an agent of life-creating power.

At the conscious level we are aware of Galileo poking his tube into the night sky in the year 1610, and sifting his observations through his reasoning mind to come up with the judgments that verified the Copernican theory of the solar-centric universe. Here the conscious mind was dealing with cosmic reality.

That the super-conscious mind is able to relate itself with some cosmic consciousness, some over-soul, some spiritual reality seems to be attested by phenomena described by Bergson, William James and other psychic researchers. Evelyn Underhill in her study of *Mysticism*, and descriptive accounts of

Edgar Cayce and other comparable phenomena, supplement these observations.

Healing processes stimulated by the great affirmations of life cannot ignore the relationships of mind and emotion that reach in the spectrum of consciousness both above and below what can be consciously controlled by the subject. Study of the phenomena of faith must push out the boundaries in both directions.

Scepticism and animal faith

Writing a generation ago, George Santayana explored the nature and content of animal faith as it bears on an understanding of man's capacity for scepticism.[1] As he develops the subject, it appears that scepticism in relation to animal faith may have much the same quality as the denial of life's meaning has upon the evidences of ill-health that we call symptoms.

With courage and clarity Santayana exposes the processes of animal faith as they relate to ordered thought and religion so that we can see more clearly some of the elements of the innate faith that we can use or impede by the processes of consciousness. Speaking of the danger of transplanting one's emotions in another, and thus losing sight of the valid emotions of the other he said, 'Philosophy fell into the same snare when in modern times it ceased to be the art of thinking and tried to become that impossible thing, the science of thought. Thought can be found only by being enacted.' Thought, then, has its meaning as a conscious process only when we realize that it is bound up with a being who embodies much more than that of which he is conscious. He further states,

> Thought is not a substitute for physical force or physical life, but an expression of them when they are working at their best. If I may read animation into nature at all, it must be where her mechanisms are sustained, not where they are suspended.

And of the power of nature to justify thought as a normal process, he writes,

Nature seems to have many levels of habit, irreducible to one another. . . As it was only the other day that a hint reached us that gravity and the first law of motion might be forms of a single principle, so it may not be long before we hear from the biologists that chemical reaction and animal instinct are forms of the same habit of matter . . . it is only my ignorance or egotism that can regard any of her ways as abnormal.

At this level, then, the

source of my confidence in animal faith, the same that inspired confidence in a child towards his parents, or toward pet animals; and the whole monstrous growth of human religion is an extension of this sense that nature is a person, or a set of persons, with constant but malleable characters. As experience remodels my impulses, I assume that the world will remain amenable to my new ways; the convert feels he is saved; the philosopher thinks he has found the key to happiness; the astronomer tells you he has measured the infinite, and perhaps rolled it up upon itself, and put it in his pocket. They all express the infantile conviction that nature cannot be false to what they have already learned or instinctively affirmed of it. . .

The inevitable result is that the limited base from which their thinking starts inevitably causes men to feel frustrated by nature as they define it. But nature is always larger than the sum of its parts, just as man is more than his mechanics or chemistry. Until this capacity for deep respect for the natural forces at work is brought to its full, the power of the innate faith at work in man will not be fully employed.

As one doctor explained to me, the average person has much greater natural recuperative power than he is aware of. The doctor knows it, and depends upon it. The physician has conscious faith in man's innate faith, so he gives him a placebo and words of encouragement. Often, in our thing-conscious

culture, the confidence that is consciously invested in the pills is all that is needed to set free the healing response of the natural forces latent and potential in all beings.

No approach to the understanding of faith in man can be adequate which does not make allowance for those important forces that are innate, inherited, racially endowed and unconscious, that have about themselves much of the momentum of life itself. Freed from the thought-produced restraints of the self-conscious being, such as fear, anxiety and frustration, these innate forces may well explain many of those phenomena that are a part of the healing process.

If we have the courage to recognize the direction which such faith takes, we may get out of its way with our guilt and fear-inducing religious concepts, and stop trying to placate imaginary personal forces in nature and rather begin to personalize the power that already exists for our use and our healing. These innate forces exist. They may be blocked or amplified by other levels of being. Ours is the task of developing adequate amplifiers.

9

Faith that is Achieved

This is no place to involve ourselves in a detailed exploration of the relation of freedom and determinism. In line with current scientific thought in other areas of life it is not unreasonable to say that man is both determined and free. There are important areas of life where it is clear to anyone that man is not free to choose: is bound by circumstance, and is obliged to adapt to conditions which he might not choose. On the other hand, there are small but important areas of life where man employs a freedom of choice that may have tremendous significance for his life.

The mechanism by which thought is conditioned, and the behaviour related to it modified, has come to prominence for a very practical reason, the threat of brain-washing. In its more intense form it presents what we consider a hazard to freedom. But in its more subtle forms we have long since adopted it as a part of everyday life. The problem seems to be not of kind but of degree. Were we to legislate against subtle suggestion with selfish purpose we can be sure that Madison Avenue would be quick to yell 'Ouch'.

Early in the struggle of philosophy to deal with the meaning of controlled thought, Leibniz, who was both philosopher and scientist, laid down the general principle that men are apt to be right in their affirmations and wrong in their negations. This was because their affirmations were built on their own experience, but their negations tended to deny the experience of others.

113

This idea, carried to its logical conclusions, could create serious difficulties for logical thought, but as a generalization it helps to give a starting point for the examination of how we can consciously control thought for clearly defined purposes.

A century ago, Emerson said, 'The education of the will is the object of our existence.' Emerson has become the patron saint of those who would employ auto-suggestion to concentrate their attention on one idea rather than another. The operating premise is that the mind is free to choose the idea upon which its attention will be focused. In auto-suggestion, certain psychological principles are employed to give direction to what is considered to be the will. Here is found the secret of a new sense of power which so many attribute to the practice of Christian Science, Faith Healing, Metaphysical Healing, New Thought and Yogi. In the education of the will it is important to keep clearly in mind certain reality factors that are at work.

If auto-suggestion is used to move the arm of a man whose motor-zone brain tissue controlling that motion is destroyed, the patient is bound to be frustrated, and as the Scripture indicates, his second condition will be worse than his first. This is not to say that there are not spiritual forces sufficient to restore the damaged tissue and restore function, but it is to say that auto-suggestion is not the method to be employed towards that end.

There are important areas where controlled thought can have its beneficial effects. William James, who did much to explore the instrumental nature of thought, and who popularized the idea of the 'will to believe', wrote sixty years ago,

> Most of us feel as if we lived habitually with a sort of cloud weighing upon us, below our highest notch of clearness in discernment, sureness in reasoning or firmness in deciding. . . We are making use of only a small part of our possible mental and physical resources. In some persons this sense of being cut off from their rightful resources is extreme and we then get the formidable neurasthenic and psychasthenic conditions, with life grown into one tissue of impossibilities. For

such persons, a modification of patterns of thought may be highly beneficial as an exercise of known psychological principles without recourse to what might be considered occult or mysterious. . . Constant repetition along normal lines of thinking or motor activity may react in a favourable manner on the nervous system, for the function makes the organ, just as much as the organ makes the function. Thus the training of the will is an important factor in psychic re-education, for the will is nothing but a selective action or reaction to certain ideas. By constant repetition, this selection can be directed into almost any channels. This is the basis of psychic and motor re-education, and educational methods are so successful because the nervous system is a plastic and not a rigid tissue.[1]

The kind of faith that is a product of development of the will may have significant influence on states of being, especially the general health of an individual, both preventatively and restoratively.

Faith that is taught and learned as knowledge

Types of knowledge can be so completely integrated into the total mental life of an individual that it can be an effective force in conditioning life at all levels of consciousness. In fact, knowledge becomes an ingredient of faith only when it is so integrated into the total life of the being that it becomes a basis for behaviour physically and emotionally as well as mentally.

An illustration may indicate this integration of knowledge into the total pattern of behaviour. When military personnel landed on Okinawa, they found little mental or emotional disturbance except as a direct result of physical injury. When children were lined up for inoculations, they appeared to feel no sensation of pain. A team of army psychologists were brought in to study the situation. . . They found a completely permissive attitude on the part of adults towards young children. Adults were almost completely enslaved to the needs and desires of

young children. They were never left alone, they were fed when they desired it, and their needs were the centre of adult attention. They grew up with the idea that it was inconceivable for an adult ever wilfully to do anything to injure a child. So they were conditioned early to be completely accepting of adults and their strong affective feelings towards children. When an adult injected a needle into a child there was no anticipation of discomfort, and so any discomfort was at a minimum. A large degree of emotional stability existed at the core of life. It was based on experience and the kind of knowledge that experience gives, but it was integrated into the rest of life so that the emotions and thoughts were conditioned by it.

This kind of knowledge is quite in contrast to what exists in other cultures, where a preoccupation with disease causes a high degree of anxiety which is an easily communicated emotion. The knowledge and the experience relating to doctors and anxiety are all mixed together in an increased sensitivity to pain and discomfort. The aggressive approach to disease is interpreted by the child as an aggressive approach to him, and he reacts with the appropriate emotions.

Trust can be learned, just as distrust can be. A father is said to have been giving his small son a basic lesson in economics. He said, 'You must learn that you cannot trust anyone.' Then he ordered his son to stand on a four-foot packing box and jump into his arms. As the boy jumped he stepped aside and said, 'See, you can't even trust your own father.' So the attitudes of adults can create or destroy trust as a basic response to life. Sometimes the basic religious attitudes of a person are a projection of the trust he has been led to expect from humans out into a larger cosmic context. If he has been injured in his early thinking, his religious response will bear the mark of the thinking either in a rational limitation or an over-compensation for the rational limitation.

It is this sort of a problem that McKellar deals with in his study of *Thinking and Imagination*.

Since religion rests on faith, it is well first to consider this

human quality. To some people 'faith' has come to mean 'believing what one knows perfectly well just isn't so'. Yet there is little reason to identify such intrinsically unrealistic, and therefore anti-scientific forms of A-thinking with what the early Christians extolled as a virtue. 'Faith' in its original sense – which it sometimes still retains – involves an attitude that need not be in the least incompatible with scientific investigations or with the acceptance of the products of logic, science and R-thinking in general. . . While faith can, of course, be misplaced, it is in itself quite compatible with reality-adjusted human thinking; and the only 'religion' which must inevitably come into conflict with science is religion conceived of as some kind of alternative to impartial and reality-adjusted thinking.

The question involved here is whether or not logical or scientific thinking as such is capable of determining what is ultimately real. The history of science is replete with instances of scientific error which for long periods of time was sustained by rigid scientific dogma.

We live so much of the time preoccupied with natural law and the conditions of the physical universe that we often ignore the function of a greater set of laws. We get to the place where we think facts are all-important. But we do not always realize that there are two levels of fact. There is the apparent reality and the ultimate reality. The apparently real is always subject to the ultimately real, even though we may not want to admit it.

For instance, men for a long time thought that the earth was flat. There was little use arguing about it, for anyone could see it was true. All you had to do was to look in any direction to establish the fact by observation. However, there came a time when the apparent fact was challenged in the name of the ultimate truth. Someone with divine imagination was able to move beyond the apparent to the true. The earth was round all the time, but men bound to the apparent did not know it.

The same thing was true with the aircraft. A year before the Wright brothers made their first flight, a learned group of

engineers declared in writing that further experiments with heavier-than-air craft were unwarranted because it had been established as a fact that such craft could not fly. The apparent fact was tested by the imagination of the Wright brothers and the essential truth was revealed.

It is not necessary to make imagination a spiritual quality to see the connection. Ultimate truth about man and his nature is not revealed by seeing him only as a physical being. Jesus refused to do this. He saw men always as potentially the sons of God, and he disciplined himself not to measure them by their apparent shortcomings, but rather by their ultimate possibilities. In Peter he saw not the weakness but the rock. In Mary he saw not the wantonness but the great capacity for devotion. In Zacchaeus he saw not the cheat but the man who wanted to find a better way.

This same ability of Jesus to deal with the essential truth rather than the apparent facts was revealed in the healing of people. He saw them not as others saw them, with the apparent truth of their diseased and crippled condition uppermost. He saw the withered arm as complete. He saw the leprous as clean. He saw the blind as responding to the light. He saw the emotionally disturbed as clothed and in their right minds. And because he was able to see the essential truth so clearly, he was able to be the channel for the faith and power that brought the divine imagination to life in the bodies of those he healed.

Creative 'seeing' is still possible. After a careful study of some so-called miraculous healings, Alexis Carrel said that the conditions could be verified by medical knowledge but could not be explained by it. He said that he had seen cancerous lesions heal before his eyes, though he could not explain how such a process could take place. Some essential truth took the place of what was apparent.

Robert Laidlaw tells of an eye to which sight was restored by spiritual therapy, though according to medical knowledge it could not function normally. But the sight is medically verified in spite of previous conditions that would tend to deny it. The essential truth again moves beyond the apparent truth.

It is in such conditions that spiritual law seems to be operative. The natural law functions within the range of the apparent, and is verified by our senses, but spiritual response to a divine imagination at work in life fulfils the requirements of the essential. Through the discipline of his spirit, and his achievement of release of spiritual power, Jesus was able to work with the essential and ultimate truth rather than with those appearances that so often pass for reality.

Faith that is taught and learned as knowledge can be a source of life-modification. It can also push back the frontiers of thought to the place where man begins to learn the ultimates instead of the symbols of the ultimates that are made known to his senses.

As never before, in our generation, men have learned that truth is revealed to them not so much by their senses as by those processes that are a part of creative thought, whereby they learn to give meaning to the insights of creative imagination. No one has ever seen an electron, an atom or a molecule. Yet no one doubts the fact that some such particles are a part of ultimate reality. Ultimate truth as it is revealed in knowledge, and as it can be taught to our higher awareness, is not bound so much to appearances as it is to the evidences of power released by it in observed experience.

Knowledge may point a way, and indicate a direction, but a broader application of the learning process is needed to integrate it. Faith can activate the knowledge we acquire. It adds the force that leads to action. Knowledge itself may be merely the clue to ultimate reality.

Faith that is felt – emotional support of knowledge

Feelings can have an important influence upon how knowledge is used. Knowledge supported by strong conviction can lead to a type of action very different from knowledge that is held with complete objectivity. Healthy or unhealthy feelings can give direction to the facts that are observed. Insignificant facts can be distorted out of all proportion so that all of life is adversely

affected if the mind is paranoid. The life that is overborne by suspicion is a living evidence of what takes place with the failure of faith. But the emotional forces that distort the facts that are observed are usually from a level of consciousness that is not easily dealt with by rational thinking alone.

The depressed person will give an entirely different meaning to the same set of facts from the person whose powers of observation are untroubled. A person with strong feelings of inferiority will turn the same facts to different meanings from those produced by the person with untroubled feelings. Emotion does things to facts.

Faith has about it a quality of emotion, for it can add a strong quality of expectancy and affirmation to life-experience. When a positive faith is added to facts, they may become the basis for strong action. This ingredient is continually at work in scientific exploration. Starting with a few facts, we may find an indication of important meaning hidden in them. Guided by a strong faith, the researcher may work with those few facts until they become a logical pattern upon which important theoretical knowledge can be built. Negatively viewed, the same facts can be discounted, and the negative force of doubt may lead the research to a quick conclusion.

Feeling in itself is not knowledge. Faith in itself does not give knowledge. But faith can so charge action with conviction and energy that the process of gaining knowledge is stimulated. It is of importance to keep a proper balance of thinking and feeling, for one without the other suffers from an important missing ingredient. The thought without the feeling may be sterile. The feeling without the thought may be meaningless. The balance of what is true with what is desired is important for scientific research, and also for the living of life.

Faith that is willed

There are times when the conscious effort to give direction to life produces a powerful act of will.

If we were aware of the way in which such acts of will could

be guaranteed, we would have solved a major psychological problem.

What Rank calls 'the psychological problem *par excellence*' is this matter of the roots of the capacity to will. Put simply, how do we will to will?

Those who approach the problem from the physico-chemical point of view say that willing is a product of organic balance. If, for instance, the thyroid glands are functioning below normal, the body is sluggish and the emotions are characterized by depression. To right the situation, thyroid extracts from the glands of sheep are taken into the human body, and the glandular balance is restored and the feelings of sluggishness and depression disappear. Therefore, the matter of willing is essentially a physico-chemical process, and when we understand all we need to know about body chemistry, we will be able to deal with the conditions of body and mind without complicated theories of how we will.

This method, however, avoids a major question. It does not face the chicken-and-egg problem that is raised concerning why the glands developed an imbalance in the first place. And the method of treatment must in some instances, at least, be approached with caution, for the problems of body balance, when taken by themselves and without regard to the basic causative factors, may become a spiral of more and more chemical agents as bodily tolerance builds up and the need for support of body mechanisms that are less and less inclined to function normally if their need is decreased by external supplements.

Those who approach the problem of willing in more mechanistic terms posit a drive so strong that it can explain the cause-effect relationships of life. Freud, for instance, tried to apply the strict determinism of natural science to psychic events, and to demonstrate the principle of causality in mental life as a response to the strongest drive he would identify, the will towards life expressed by the sex drive conceived in its largest sense.

Here again the explanation is self-limiting because it does

not adequately cover all of the circumstances of life as it is lived by the self-conscious, God-conscious individual. While such a theory has done much to illuminate the nature of man and his drives, it is not a large enough theory to encompass all that man is.

In his efforts to include the insights of Freud but seek a larger meaning for life itself Rank searched the philosophical and anthropological roots of meaning of life. Starting with life itself he says, 'The single real obstacle which freedom of will encounters is death, which it conquers by spiritual belief.' Mana to the primitive is this spirit life which can exist among the living who have great strength of spirit, or among the dead, who can use it to haunt or help. Among primitives, mana was a form of psychic energy. Its wonder-working counterpart in sustaining life is recorded in the visits to the children of Israel in their long and hungry trek.

The *Encyclopedia Britannica* speaks of it as 'magical power invested in individuals whose wills rule the universe.' Yet some such theory in more acceptable guise has appeared in most of the non-deterministic world views. It underlay the Platonic world-soul, the Hellenistic doctrine of pneuma, Schelling's romantic nature-soul, Aristotle's doctrine of body and soul, Leibniz's doctrine of the monad, and modern vitalism. Such a mystical theory in science shows up in the quantum theory.

Among primitives it was assumed that death would never be the result of natural causes, and so it must be the result of control of the life of the individual by some force beyond the individual, usually an evil force. The struggle to overcome this evil power was projected in theories of immortality, and the continued life of the spirit.

Theories of sin, guilt and atonement have their roots in the need to placate evil spiritual forces that may possess life, and to win the approval of good spirits that guarantee a good life. The offering of blood sacrifices was a symbolic giving of self and individuality to the community of the dead in order to protect the right to go on living.

The concept of God in primitive societies is diffused and

invested in a number of the mana-bearing spirits. Only with man's more complete understanding of the mystery of sex, and the form of immortality that was a part of reproduction, did the idea of God acquire fatherly qualities.

Yet even this fatherly God-idea demanded blood sacrifice in order that life might be preserved, but here the preservation was not in an individuality of spirit so much as it was in the achievement of a resurrection experience for the mass soul of mankind. It is difficult for us to understand the impact of early Christianity upon its rather primitive thought-patterns apart from this achievement of victory over the frightening spectre of death itself. But this is achieved not so much through divine manipulation as it is done through an achievement of a new idea of what life itself means.

So Jesus as the only-begotten Son was given that man might know the meaning of life. This life was to be more abundant than the frightened experience of the past, for its basis was in unity with a God of love. However, it was not an easy unity. It was bought at a price. The restoration of health was a symbol of this process, and the raising from the dead of common men was its main evidence. The final proof of the ultimate value of the spiritual achievement of God in man was the willing acceptance of death in order to prove once and for all that it was not to be feared even in its most cruel form. So the disciples, full of the courage for life that came with the realization of the meaning of the life and death of Jesus, were filled with a new will to live and make all of life subject to this power that could overcome even death. 'O death, where is thy sting? O grave, where is thy victory?' But the price of the victory is paid again and again in every generation by those who give themselves to divine will, for there is no other way under heaven in which it can be done. This divine will is shown in the life and example of Jesus.

This achievement of will and its ultimate freedom is won, paradoxically, by a denial of will, of self-will in favour of divine-will.

So this faith that is willed is an achievement of mystical unity

with the beyond-self. It does not deny reason but it is not bound by it. It has about its nature the super-rational. Any chemical or deterministic explanation of the faith that is willed must fall far short of dealing with the totality of man. The faith that is willed always demands more than reason can justify.

'All things whatsoever you pray and ask for, believe that you will receive them; then you shall have them.' This involves more than reason and logic. It involves a tremendous act of will. But it is a will projected on the premise that what man seeks, the divine consciousness is already more anxious to give than man is to receive. Here it becomes not so much a matter of knowing faith as a process of generating the response of faith that produces results. 'By faith Abraham went out', 'Stretch forth thy hand', 'Go, wash in the pool of Siloam', 'Show thyself to the priest', 'You have answered right, This do and you shall live.' The natural mind is inclined to ask, 'Why?' The mind that is subject to a spiritual power that is involved in the will of faith, is satisfied with a great affirmation, 'Yes, Lord.'

This, logically, brings us to the place where we examine the faith that is revealed.

10

Mystical Illumination and the Superhealthy Person

We have looked at the type of faith that is built-in by innate pattern, instinctive response or unconscious conditioning.

We have looked at the kind of faith that is achieved through knowledge, conviction and the mysterious process we call an act of will.

Now let us look at the level of faith that may build on the other two, but instead of being primarily rooted in the lower or conscious level of the mental life, employs the higher levels of consciousness for its purposes.

Thinking about the super-conscious areas of mental activity is as speculative as examination of the unconscious. There are small windows by which we can get glimpses of the kind of mental activity that takes place in both directions, but it is important always to keep in mind that we are projecting theories. However, theories need to be projected in order to be tested, and tested in order to make the basis for more adequate theories.

For our purposes we will think of the phenomena relating to the super-conscious as falling into three categories, the psychological, the psychic, and the parapsychic. The psychological is entirely within the person and can be explained largely by deductive reasoning. The psychic involves the minds of others with whom there is some kind of a response and communication. The parapsychic begins with the mind of the subject, but involves a form of cosmic consciousness or revelation that

cannot be explained on psychological grounds or on the basis of communication with the mind of another person.

The Aztecs used mescaline to induce mystical states. In modern experiments with mescaline it is shown that only some persons react to the drug by a mystical state. Similar states can be induced by inhaling nitrous oxide. Under these influences a person seems to be released from the measurements and restraints of reality and his mind soars into states of unusual colour, beauty and grandeur. The mind seems to be set free at the same time that it is given the power for great inner assent.

Similar states come to those intoxicated by alcohol, or opium and its derivatives, or those who may have created a toxic condition in the blood due to long periods of fasting or lack of sleep. The lower the bodily strength or energy factor, the higher appears to be the susceptibility to this kind of emotional stimulation.

Early in the history of the church it was found that such mystical states could be cultivated, and excesses resulted as would-be saints competed with each other for more magnificent visions. The spurious nature of the results of such methods became dangerous for the life of the church and such excesses were frowned upon.

One of the expressions of this form of experience is that it is difficult to communicate it or translate it into words. Often some other form of medium is used in an effort at communication. The arts are often the product of the ecstatic emotional responses of the artist. Coleridge tried to put into poetry a vision that came to him in an opium dream, and Kubla Khan embodies something of his own reaction to the visions he was able to capture in words.

The main characteristic of this type of experience is a release, whatever the mechanisms of the release may be. One characteristic of the mystical reaction is an impression of increased insight, whether real or apparent. Evidence seems to contradict the view that such insight is invariably false. The release often produces extremes of certainty that are unwarranted when tested by reality. Often desire seems to be the artisan at work to

shape the dream, which with its sense of certainty then fortifies the desire. Also, these mystical states have an echo when the mental processes return to the atmosphere of normal reality-tested thought. This probably explains much superstitious behaviour, where although people consciously refuse to believe that there could be any adverse effect from walking under a ladder, they still will refuse to do it, 'just because'.

Psychologically explained phenomena account for many of the conditions that present themselves to those examining the mystical experience. It is important for our purposes to know just as clearly what is not a real mystical experience as what is, for much confusion has developed even among well-qualified observers because they were unable to establish categories to sharpen their thinking.

Psychic awareness adds another area of consideration to the study of the phenomena of mysticism. After considerable independent research on the subject Alexis Carrel wrote,

> Clairvoyance and telepathy are a primary datum of scientific observation. Those endowed with this power grasp the secret thoughts of other individuals without using their sense organs. They also perceive events more or less remote in space and time. This quality is exceptional. It develops in only a small number of human beings. But many possess it in a rudimentary state. They use it without effort and in a spontaneous fashion. Clairvoyance appears quite common-place to those having it. It brings to them a knowledge which is more certain than that gained through the sense organs. A clairvoyant reads the thoughts of other people as easily as he examines the expression of their faces. But the words to see and to feel do not accurately express the phenomena taking place in his consciousness. He does not observe, he does not think. He knows.[1]

Clairvoyance which means clear seeing, when employed by a person who does not know the meaning of the phenomena at work in him, can easily be interpreted in terms of a belief that he is subject to a mystical revelation.

Dora VanGelder, a psychic diagnostician, has worked with O. J. Bengtsson, MD, in New York for many years. She claims that in their many years of association she has never given a medically inaccurate diagnosis, but has often perceived conditions of the body psychically which were not accessible to ordinary diagnostic procedures. Under examination by four psychiatrists at a Wainwright House seminar, Dora VanGelder tried to interpret the phenomena that occur during her activities of a diagnostic nature. She says that she tries to see the person in question, not primarily with her physical eyes but with a kind of second sight which focuses on an electromagnetic field that surrounds each person. Colours emanating from various parts of the body vary from bright, healthy colours to dull, drab unhealthy colours. This can be done with eyes closed. The unhealthy colour is traced to its source, and the location described to the doctor who then uses medical methods of verifying the diagnosis.

This appears to be a type of clairvoyance where a person with special gifts organizes and employs psychic energies for the purposes described. The phenomena employ the energies of one living body in such a way that the person with psychic gifts is sensitive to them, but it is primarily a relationship of person to person.

This sort of response of the energy field of one person to the energy field of another is perhaps a more common phenomena than we assume. Sorokin has projected the theory that the genius personality is one with psychic gifts, whether he is aware of them or not. These gifts make it possible for him to have instantaneous knowledge where other persons have to go through the more normal channels in acquiring their knowledge.

Carrel tries to make a working distinction at this point.

Men of genius, in addition to their powers of observation and comprehension, possess other qualities, such as intuition and creative imagination. Through intuition they learn things ignored by other men, they perceive relations between seem-

ingly isolated phenomena, they unconsciously feel the presence of the unknown treasure. All great men are endowed with intuition. They know without analysis, without reasoning, what is important for them to know. . . This phenomenon, in former times, was called inspiration. . . Certainty derived from science is very different from that derived from faith. The latter is more profound. It cannot be shaken by argument. It resembles the certainty given by clairvoyance. But, strange to say, it is not completely foreign to science. Obviously, great discoveries are not the product of intelligence alone.[2]

If this sort of process is at work in the discoveries of the scientist whose thinking is continually reality-tested, it is perhaps even more of a factor in the creative effort of the artist whose work is measured more by its imaginative quality. As a child I remember questioning the sister-in-law of Rachmaninoff at great length about the way he worked when he was composing. She told me that he would go into the woods and sit on a rock or a stump for hours at a time with his pencil and score pad. Sometimes nothing would happen, and at other times he would pour out upon paper a flood of those symbols of sound that are the stock and trade of the composer. Then he would hurry home to try it on the piano to see what had come to him. It is quite certain that Rachmaninoff took something more into the woods than his paper and pencil. The average person, going apart like that, would not be apt to produce anything of musical value. The creative element was within the artist, and the special circumstances helped to break it loose.

These phenomena that can be psychologically explained, or that are the product of special mental gifts, such as clairvoyance, telepathic sensitivity, or the qualities of the creative genius, are not enough to explain certain conditions that seem to exist when the mind of a human achieves illumination, or is subject to divine intrusion, or what we might call the visitation of the Holy Spirit. Let us be clear, many of the phenomena that religious persons have thought were evidences of the indwelling of the

Holy Spirit could be explained by a lesser agency. If we are to isolate the true revelation, we must make sure that we are not cluttering up the picture with tricks our minds can play on us.

If the revelation of God is the highest form of faith of which man can be aware, he does not want that high knowledge to be the product of illusion or confusion.

When we deal with the revelations of the human mind for which there is no reasonable psychological explanation and for which no other human agency seems to be employed, we immediately run into the possibility of the influence of a discarnate entity, human in origin, but having experienced what we call physical death. Here evidence of both the British and American Societies for Psychical Research seems to sustain the theory that some portion of the human consciousness is able for a period of time to carry on some form of independent existence, and under certain conditions to establish meaningful communication with persons yet alive. The mechanisms by which this is done remain largely unknown, but it appears to be a form of energy comparable to the electromagnetic field that surrounds the human body, which disengages itself from the human body at death and continues an independent existence for a lesser or greater period of time. When the electro-magnetic field of a living being is 'porous' or susceptible to intrusion, the energy of the discarnate entity appears to penetrate into the being of the living person, and he becomes a medium through which the self-conscious intelligence of the discarnate entity is expressed. This intrusion from the realm of discarnate beings cannot easily be considered an invasion of the Holy Spirit, nor can the insights derived therefrom be given the status of divine revelations, for the human agency, in whatever form it manifests itself, is still the important factor.

The idea of divine revelation is avoided by many because it is beyond easy modes of thought. But within man's nature there seem to be meeting places for elements of reality that are larger than the measuring sticks we hold to them. This inclination to be afraid of what we cannot control by measurement seems to be deep seated in the emotions of men, even those who are

devoted to scientific procedures. When the news of the invention of the telephone was reported to Professor Tait, of Edinburgh, he said, 'It is all humbug, for such a discovery is physically impossible.' When the Abbé Moignon first showed Edison's phonograph to the Paris Academy of Sciences, all the men of science present declared it impossible to reproduce the human voice by means of the metal disc, and the Abbé was accused, Sir William Barrett tells us, of having a ventriloquist concealed beneath the table. The thing was unbelievable. If such mechanical phenomena have been subject to the rejection of the learned because of their fear of careful investigation of their own prejudice, how much more so is it probable that the phenomena bearing on the rare characteristics of the human mind would be discredited?'

The nature of true revelation moves beyond the doubts of man, and the phenomena of self-realization and communication to a quality of relationship which Gerald Heard calls 'higher prayer', and Richard Maurice Bucke, a psychiatrist who himself experienced the revelation, calls it the 'cosmic consciousness.' The phenomenon, rare in nature, appears as a form of illumination, where insight into the nature of being and the relationships of being flood the consciousness and lead to action on the basis of the consciousness. George Washington Carver talked with peanuts and then listened, and there was revealed to him knowledge about the secret structure of matter that he was able to act upon.

Einstein shared such an experience, and he described it in his little book *Cosmic Religion*.

The religious geniuses or all time have been distinguished by this cosmic religious sense, which recognizes neither dogmas nor God made in man's image. . . How can this cosmic religious experience be communicated from man to man if it cannot lead to a definite conception of God or to a theology? It seems to be that the most important function of art and of science is to arouse and keep alive this feeling in those who are receptive. . . Only those who have dedicated their lives to

similar ends can have a living conception of the inspiration which gave these men the power to remain loyal to their purpose in spite of countless failures. It is the cosmic religious sense which grants this power. A contemporary has rightly said that the only deeply religious people of our largely materialistic age are the earnest men of research.[3]

So it would seem that this kind of mental activity is a form of power, that it not only comes from a contemplation of ultimate reality, but in some way brings the mind of the contemplator into an active and illuminating relationship with that ultimate reality, It can be blocked by dogmas and selfish anthropomorphisms, and it can be released by an openness, a humility and a selflessness that is the characteristic of the truth-seeking mind, whether it be scientific or religious, for ultimately both are the same. And both produce an illumination which can be tested by time and life and found to be in accord with reality. In this way revealed truth is a part of all truth, and if it has any special significance it has it not because it is more true, but because of the method by which the truth was made known to the mind of man.

New light on the super-conscious

Our understanding of the psychological, the psychic and the parapsychic has been sharpened in recent years by the careful work of many researchers who have examined the phenomena of the human mind and its function.

Some of this research has had to do with the way the mind works. As I mentioned in the introduction to these pages, the work of scientists like Lord Adrian has helped us to understand the brain as an energy-producing piece of equipment. Brain waves can be measured, and it has been computed that with a properly adjusted transformer and the brain working at full energy creating capacity, enough power would be developed to run a five watt transmitter. At the short wave bands this energy output would be able to send signals quite a distance.

Some of these studies have made the problem of consciousness seem more difficult. A sharp uppercut to the jaw can send a boxer into a state of unconsciousness. Yet when careful experiments were carried on at Johns Hopkins Medical School to try to locate the centre of consciousness, it appeared to be elusive. By electric shock various areas of brain tissue were made temporarily inoperative. Portion after portion of the brain was blocked off without affecting consciousness. Only two small areas were isolated which had direct bearing on consciousness. Brain surgeons indicate that large portions of brain tissue can be excised without affecting normal mental activity or consciousness. Physicians report accidental injury and war-inflicted injuries which have involved massive areas of brain tissue without apparently affecting consciousness.

This thing we call mind may not be as closely bound up with physiological function as was once supposed. While the relationship of brain and thought, mental activity and consciousness, can be demonstrated, it is also possible to demonstrate that the variety and complexity of mental activity involves something more than physiological functioning. This may explain the ability of the consciousness to persist after death. Such records as that of his own experience addressed to the Royal Medical Society by Sir Auckland Geddes, while too lengthy to reproduce, may be read in detail to show how the consciousness with its attendant mental activities can be carried on in apparent separation from the body.

Studies like those of Schmeidler and McConnell, published by Yale University Press, who set out to discredit once and for all the premise and methods of research in telepathy, are especially significant. After fifteen years of careful work, Schmeidler, a psychologist, and McConnell, a physicist-mathematician, arrived at results that not only supported previous research by other investigators, but added original theoretical understanding. By dividing those who believed and disbelieved, before testing, they were able to compare results, and found that those who believed in a telepathic capacity scored as significantly above chance as those who disbelieved scored

below chance. So the power of disbelief appears to be a measurable factor, just as the power of belief is. In other correlations they found that the intelligence quotient of the person has a bearing on his telepathic capacity, and that the higher the intelligence quotient, the higher the scoring on tests. Also significant in their work was a correlation of personality types with scoring, and it was found that rigid, rejecting and negative personality types scored low, while responsive, out-going persons scored higher.

There are definitely types of person who are more responsive to paranormal manifestations. These persons are undoubtedly more apt to be responsive to revealed faith as it would be consciously observed, and they too would probably be more responsive to certain types of healing that might be the result of psychological, psychic or parapsychic agency.

The creative consciousness

The same sort of a problem that existed with the will to believe exists with the creative consciousness. What is the explanation of the willingness to make the effort towards such a state of mind, and what is the relation of the willing to the endowment which a person may possess? Any answers are tentative and speculative.

Traditionally there has been a belief that such states could be cultivated. Ancient practice was to go apart, and preferably up to a high place. The Tibetans and the Peruvians and other high-dwelling persons seemed to cultivate such a consciousness. Whether this is a result of psychological suggestion and a kinesthetic pull, or whether it is due to the lack of oxygen in the higher altitudes, or whether it might be due to an increase in the effects of cosmic radiation, is still but a matter of conjecture. Fruitful research at these points might prove to be helpful.

Religious practice traditionally justified such efforts as height reaching for height. Yet the end-result usually seems to be that the revelation comes not from the thunder, and lightning, the wind and the storm, exhilarating though they may be, but

rather from the depths of the being, the still, small voice, to which one may more easily respond in quietness and in isolation.

This cultivated capacity for quiet listening may be an important prerequisite for the revelation of truth from within. So the painter sitting before his canvas hour after hour is listening to something within himself that wants to speak. It may be something sifting up from the deep levels of consciousness, or something sifting down from the superconscious. Certainly the creative consciousness would be characterized by both.

Psychic awareness

A variety of persons interested in the phenomena of the superconscious have indicated how they think the responsive state may be attained. Writers like Gerald Heard and Douglas V. Steere have written about it as a form of prayer. Medical men from James Esdaile to Lewis Wolberg have indicated how the state of suggestion that leads to hypnotic responsiveness can be cultivated. Psychical researchers like Hornell Hart and Eileen Garrett have given directions for the cultivating of a state of mind and emotion that is conducive to the responses of a psychic nature. Arthur Ford, the sensitive who broke the Houdini code, has given his prescription for the kind of procedure that can be followed to develop psychic sensitivity. All approach the subject as if they were dealing with quite natural phenomena that could be developed by directed effort.

Cultivating revealed truth

Let us look at some of the methods they suggest for the creating of mental susceptibility to the revealed forms of truth.

All seem to agree that there are certain external conditions to be cultivated. Silence, alone or in a group, is important. So are certain external circumstances that may be rich in suggestion, such as a chapel, a place of beauty, or a place invested with meaning by the spiritual activity of others. Symbolism appears

to be an important factor in creating sensitivity and thought direction.

Relaxation is another universally recommended state. It involves not only the deliberate and carefully directed relaxation of the muscles of the body, especially those that gather tension like the diaphragm and the lower jaw, but also relaxation of the emotions so that they are freed from the tensions of anxiety, fear, and worry. Also, it is important to relax the mind so that while thought is possible, the mind is freed from strenuous effort.

Esdaile and Wolberg state that the feeling of ready cooperation and willingness to accept suggestion is important for their processes which are more definitely hypnotic. However, Hart, Garrett and Ford feel it is important to achieve a state of ready responsiveness somewhere near the edge of consciousness, as if it were possible to slip into the superconscious state just as it is possible to slip into the subconscious state. We are told that it is in such a state that most dreaming takes place, at least those dreams that can be recalled. So also it seems to be that visions of truth and spiritual insight come in such a peripheral condition.

Into these states, where the burdens of consciousness are partly eased, the insights are received, and translated into the normal symbolism of language. Much of this kind of conditioning has long been a part of the preparation for worship and prayer. The mystics have employed such techniques through the ages. Modern study of the mind and its processes verifies the insight that has come out of the long practice of those who practised more than they knew.

Further elaboration of these methods will be undertaken when we deal with the techniques of prayer. Here it is sufficient to point out that members of the disciplined professions corroborate the methods that tradition has employed. Spiritual sensitivity can be cultivated, and the conditions that may lead to the kind of faith that is revealed may be as much strenuous discipline as it is some peculiar sensitivity.

11

Cultivating the Release Mechanisms

We have spent some time looking at what faith is when examined in depth. It is a response to life which employs the innate, the achieved and the revealed, so that the power of God may be at work in man.

Now we come to a description of what it is that faith does when it is at work in the being.

Dr Eugene Smith, who heads the foreign missions programmes of a large denomination of Protestantism, affirms that it was a psychoanalytic process that was the source of spiritual revelation to him, and the processes of revelation were very closely bound up with the processes that released him from restraints on love and understanding and free him for a more useful and productive way of life.

If the processes of faith employ something comparable to the insight of the artist, it is quite clear that they are well employed if they make of living the greatest of the fine arts. For although all truth is one, there are differing dimensions by which truth seems to be measured. The truth of mathematics may be more exact but less satisfying than the truth of wholeness of being in response to great life-affirmations. The truth that releases life is not bound by small and destructive measurements, but rather is the stuff of which true freedom is made. But as the psychoanalytic process is not a quick and easy way to truth about the self, so also the truth of faith that sets life free is not usually achieved in a quick and easy manner. The grasping of the higher levels of God-consciousness within the person is often stimulated by

the type of personal example that is found in a person like Jesus of Nazareth, who with psychic awareness, and personal discipline, achieved a free flow of the power that faith releases in life, so that those who heard his words were stimulated to realize their own possibilities, those who felt his healing touch knew a power that went to the depth of their infirmity, and those who learned his methods of life were able to appropriate for themselves a power that modified the world as long as they were alive to use it. But the power of the faith that releases seemed to have been largely lost with them. If we would recapture it as a force for life we will need to look at where it was seen last.

Yet the remnants of this faith that releases life can still be applied, and the evidences of it are visible in the lives of persons who employ it even to a limited degree. Often this faith is expressed in those preliminary efforts to turn back the tide of destructive thought-processes. It is characterized by a power to set life free from the false limits that persons place upon themselves. It is the faith that helps people to get out of their own way. In doing that it helps to determine which self is going to have ascendancy in life. Often this is done through a faith that releases persons from false feelings of guilt.

The false limits upon life are usually shown by an inability to make decisions, strong feelings of self-condemnation that inhibit creative action, feelings of unworthiness and a life characterized by a succession of emotional crises that grow from conflicting feelings.

The faith that releases tends to go to work at the lower level of consciousness to generate the understanding of self and others that breaks up the emotional log-jam. Sometimes this is done as a reaction to the infinite patience shown by a psychoanalyst in leading a person to look more objectively at the self and the selves. At other times it happens as a result of a religious experience that serves as a catalytic agent in the deep emotions. Sometimes the danger here is that destructive patterns of behaviour are congealed by the supposed sanction of religious feelings. Often the process is a part of a gradual modification of life due to the impact of experience and the learning process.

Release from anxiety and worry

Much of the emotional energy of life is used up by persons who are anxious and worried. Anxiety is characterized by an inability to take constructive action about a situation that is causing injury to life. It has been said that most of the things we worry about never happen, and even if they did happen, our worry would not do any good. In fact the worry keeps a person off balance enough to make it difficult for him to meet situations with his best intelligence and energy.

There is a reasonable place for fear in life. It is the basis of much learning, and progress in nutrition is due to fear of starvation, progress in building is due to fear of the elements, and fear of disease has stimulated much medical progress. But when fear becomes a way of life, and things are feared which are not fearful, some deep-seated habit of thought needs to be regrooved. Sometimes we learn bad habits of thought, and sometimes they are forced upon us by circumstance. The natural basic response to life is not characterized by unreasonable fears.

Those superficial approaches to life's problems that seem to indicate that wishing can make it so tend to employ a half-truth. The response to the half-truth may give temporary benefits that will inspire confidence in a person. Putting on rose-coloured glasses may make drab objects look more colourful, but the only thing that is changed is the visual experience of the beholder. The object remains the same. If a person is walking towards a pit, rose-coloured glasses will not keep him from falling into it, but may even precipitate a fall. There is real danger in the misuse of psychological principle. The approach to religion as a form of life-manipulation is superficial, and the results will be superficial. Some persons may find temporary or even long-term removal of symptoms from such superficial processes, but the basic wholeness of being is not so apt to be involved.

Rollo May points out that anxiety is a distorted concern for the future based on an accumulation of free-floating fear that has become congealed in the present. Often it shows itself in

false ideas about important aspects of life. In his study of Martin Luther, Erik Erikson points out that certain things that happened to Luther early in life had long-term effects upon him. Cruel assaults upon his buttocks by punitive parents characterized his early discipline. This produced a deep sense of guilt which conflicted with a strong desire for justice. The problem plagued his early years, and finally the stored-up aggressiveness broke loose in revolt against the adult symbols of parental authority. Because the time was propitious and Luther was a man of great ability, an important historical event took place. Sometimes right things are done for the wrong reasons, and sometimes wrong things are done for the right reasons.

Sometimes the anxiety-stimulated ideas attach to problems that were acute before the level of conscious recollection was achieved. David W had feeding difficulties when he was a few weeks old. His mother could not continue to nurse him, and a satisfactory substitute was not found. For weeks the emotional states of all concerned were disturbed. Now as an adult David is a food faddist. He reads every label on every food container, he questions his wife about ingredients in food, he is distressed about food additives, and writes to Congress regularly about modification of laws to protect persons from poison sprays, artificial colourings and flavours, and in general projects a great deal of anxiety into the matter of eating. He is thinking of giving up a good position to start a small farm so that he can be sure of having the right kinds of food for himself and his family. Free-floating anxiety traced to an early experience seems to be the cause of present behaviour patterns.

In understanding the faith that releases, it is important on the one hand to appreciate the powerful forces at work for normality within the being, and on the other the nature and significance of the emotional factors that block these forces. Because many of them are at low levels of consciousness, it is also important to understand the techniques that are employed for modification and release. Some of the techniques have nothing to do with what we have traditionally thought of as religion, though in its larger definition, nothing that has to do

with the release of spiritual power in life should be excluded from the realm of the religious. Perhaps some of the confusion in evaluating certain religious groups and cults develops at this point. They have found effective techniques for life release apart from the traditional modes of religious practice. Because they are not traditional, they are unacceptable to the traditionally-minded. However, they need to be studied objectively in order to understand what they are and what they can do.

A couple of generations ago Mary Baker Eddy, with skill in organization and strong personal appeal, presented the idea of Christian Science. It was attacked as being both theologically and philosophically unsound, but large numbers of persons found that in spite of these criticisms it was able to do for them what they needed done. Charles Raynolds Brown, Dean of Yale Divinity School, undertook a study of the phenomena and as a result wrote a book of real psychological insight. He called it *The Healing Power of Suggestion*. The substance of this book was that although it might be theologically and philosophically unsound, the movement of Christian Science had made available to people a psychologically sound principle that was changing their lives. This principle was characterized by repetitious creative affirmation. It was effective in replacing hate with love, fear with faith and illness with health.

A generation ago a Frenchman, Coué, created a stir with the idea of effective auto-suggestion. Large numbers of persons found that they felt better, more cheerful and worked better if they started the day by repeating a number of times, 'Every day in every way I am getting better and better.' Most persons made no effort to comprehend the deeper meanings of what Dr Coué was talking about, and so the accepting took a superficial dose of his verbal medicine and felt better for a while, and the others who paid any attention at all criticized and ridiculed, but still were baffled by the rather obvious results that were attained even by a superficial practice of these psychological techniques.

More recently, both within and outside the orthodox church, there has been an awareness of the effectiveness of such techniques.

In a number of cities where downtown churches have been struggling for their life against indifference and shifting populations, the exponents of New Thought have been filling opera houses and music halls during the week and on Sundays, with a simple presentation in more erudite and scientifically acceptable tones of these same ideas that speak directly to the release mechanisms of the lower levels of consciousness.

Among the more orthodox churches, men like Dr Norman Vincent Peale have found a ready response to their message of rather repetitive affirmations concerning life which seem inane to the conscious mind as it evaluates them, but which seem effectively to reach the jammed-up areas of the lower levels of consciousness with effective release mechanisms.

Starting with the more intellectually respectable presentation of these techniques in such books as Hornell Hart's *Auto-Conditioning*, and Kinnear's *The Creative Power of the Mind*, and moving down the line through the variety of books and pamphlets that suggest techniques, all have in common one basic premise, and that is that there are conscious patterns of thought and action that can reach and modify the lower reaches of consciousness. Dr Hart says that those who master the technique he recommends will never again have to be faced with a state of depression. Others talk about facing each new day with a sense of victorious achievement. A publisher who specializes in such literature confided privately that he felt guilty about publishing such books, for they tend to take unfair advantage of the three million obsessive-compulsive neurotics who are the book-buying segment of the population towards which they are aimed, but as he added laconically, 'such books carry the rest of our list'.

The obsessive-compulsive neurotic is characterized by a deep-seated fear of life and a need for perpetual reassurance. His insecure inner world will totter and fall if it is not continually shored up by some support from the outside. So he turns to those sources of assurance that day by day and week by week tell him that life is not so bad and he is not so threatened. So he gets through his days 'sustained and soothed by a faltering

trust', but one that can be renewed whenever needed by getting to the right place or the right person quickly enough.

The traditional emphasis of the church on daily devotions and Bible reading had much the same effect when actually employed. Starting the day with great affirmations such as 'This is the day that the Lord hath made, let us rejoice and be glad in it', or 'Ye are the sons of God, and if sons then joint heirs' would inevitably give a greater significance to both the external and the internal world. The bases for anxiety and fear would be swallowed up in a truth large enough to sustain life, whatever the incidents of life might be.

This brings us to the point where we must evaluate these various emphases. They have in common a direct approach to the lower levels of consciousness where the emotional conditions lurk that can lay waste life. It is important to meet the needs of people at this level, to release them from the life-crippling effects of anxiety and worry. But it is also important to employ release mechanisms that can minister to the whole of life. Merely to use the emotional state of the obsessive-compulsive neurotic, for instance, as a point of control over the mind and emotions of the individual for selfish purposes, is an intolerable trespassing on the sacred precincts of personality.

As Charles R. Brown pointed out more than a generation ago, the orthodox church must have a ministry to persons who have personality needs so deep that they crave techniques that reach the depths of their beings. However, if the church is to be worthy of its traditional regard for the total personality of man as made in the image of God, it cannot consciously justify the employment of techniques that reinforce the emotional state of those who have a diseased consciousness. Rather, it must so minister to the deep needs of the person that they will be moved beyond the processes of temporary restoration to that wholeness of being which will bring true life fulfillment. In other words, instead of merely treating the symptoms, it will treat the diseased consciousness from which the symptoms spring. The employment of psychological techniques toward this end finds its justification in the goal as well as the method. The repetition

of great affirmations as a psychological method which weakens the reality sense at the same time that it salves the deeply-injured consciousness is hardly warranted. The method must stimulate release at all levels of being without injury to any part of the consciousness if it is to be worthy of the high valuation we would put on the human soul.

So in resolving the deep roots of anxiety it is not enough to repeat endlessly, 'Be not anxious.' It is equally important to point out that there are great spiritual resources for the sustaining of life that are adequate to release the being from its fears, for 'Do you not know that your heavenly Father knoweth that you have need of these things.' The cosmic consciousness sustains all the rest of being without illusion. To see and be made aware of man's status in creation undergirds the affirmations of life with a sense of ultimate reality that cannot be outgrown.

Release from meaninglessness

In establishing the larger premise for the overcoming of anxiety and worry it is important to do more than regroove the thought patterns that affect the lower levels of consciousness. It is important to release the strength of life through bringing to life its essential meaning. Philosophy has wrestled with this problem of the meaningfulness of life. In his *The Philosophy of 'As If'*, Hans Vahinger projects the idea that acting as if something were true makes it true for the individual who projected the idea. The thesis is that truth is an experienced reality on the part of the individual. This same idea has been central in the thought of William James, who expressed the pragmatic idea that if a thing works it is true, at least for those who work it. John Dewey developed the instrumental nature of truth in his philosophy of education, where learning is essentially the product of doing, directly or indirectly. Such ideas are not foreign to existentialism with its emphasis of the ultimate reality of being, with truth as the experience of being in the encounter with the matrix of life

which weaves together the subjective and the objective in an inseparable unity.

The experience of being is empty and frustrating if the struggle is unwarranted by adequate purpose. How often in the counselling room the core of the problem of an individual comes out with a sigh and such words as, 'Oh, if I could only find a meaning to it all.' 'The endless, meaningless routine is driving me mad. Dishes and dishes, meals and meals, dirt and dirt, and no end to it all. What good is life if that is all it is?'

Those who would merely condition the lower levels of consciousness would use mechanisms of release that would say that it is as easy to attribute meaning to life as it is meaninglessness. Just attribute meaning to the endless routine and it takes on meaning. Meaning gives more meaning just as doubt feeds doubt.

The approach to meaning that not only brings release at the lower levels of consciousness but also sustains and fulfils the totality of being would deal with the affirmation that the power of God is at work in life to make it good. Just as the built-in wisdom works to heal the cut finger without the intervention of conscious effort, so the built-in meaningfulness of life is continually at work to give value to existence, and the dampening effect of a perverted consciousness that poisons the wells of being with unreasoned doubt needs to be purified not by psychological devices alone, but by a reawakened awareness of the power of God at work to bring life to its finest fulfilment.

Then the meaning of life is not something that we make but something that we realize. Like the pattern in a crystal, or the design in a scallop shell, or the sense of destiny in a salmon or the responsiveness of a homing pigeon, man's nature is to realize the full measure of his God-consciousness. This realization saturates the lower levels of consciousness with purpose as it opens the upper levels of consciousness with responsiveness. And the reality is not a partial thing that can lead to frustration if it is not given its daily ration of assurance, but rather draws on a deeper consciousness of life's meaning to move beyond the

realms of easy frustration to the deeper consciousness of the unity of all life with its divine creative origin.

The power to release is within

When the full spiritual consciousness is realized, the deeper levels of being are brought into accord with the highest levels of consciousness. The processes may vary from analytic awareness, through the processes of slow maturing to the quick revelation of conversion. But whatever it is, it brings an awareness of power waiting to be released, and the consciousness of this power removes doubt and fear, weakness and a sense of personal failure.

Too often we seek for our assurance in material power. It is never there except as a supplement and tool of the power that is realized from within.

When Jesus stood before Pilate, he was in the presence of the symbol of the power of a great political empire. Pilate was invested with earthly authority that involved life or death. But he was reminded by Jesus that this was a secondary power. Jesus said in effect, 'You have no power over me except as I grant it to you.' Here is the ultimate assurance of life, so secure in its inner relationships that the incidents of life are truly incidental, and the inner reserves of meaning are so complete that they define and limit the influence of external circumstance upon these reserves of meaning.

The power of true release is from within. It may be approached by psychological devices and easy formulas of repetition, but they are always the symptoms of the real power that is waiting to be released when the full meaning of life is realized. The power of release is from within. It is involved both as an act of faith and as a response to an act. This may at first seem impossible, but when we realize that we are dealing with two mechanisms it may be understood. The conscious faith is an act of consciousness, and the unconscious response to the act of faith is a release of energy at the innate or built-in level of being. The equipment of faith is built into life and is waiting to be

released by a mental activity that consciously cooperates with this reservoir of innate power of being.

At the conscious level of experience the great deterrent to the full realization of this power grows from the misuse of freedom. As the parable of Adam and Eve has shown, the temptation to use freedom for limited self-interest invariably starts a person down the road to limited living. The insight of the New Testament designation of Jesus as a second Adam is related to the belief that Jesus was the first individual to so use the freedom of choice that was his that he not only released his innate spiritual power, but also supplemented it with the conscious freedom of choice which in turn kept the channels open for the full realization of the superconscious indwelling of the Holy Spirit.

Perhaps the greatest of man's fears is the fear of his own inner spiritual power. It is so powerful that he is afraid he would not be able to control it. It is important for its full release to realize that the control mechanism of faith at its fullest is also a part of his willing surrender of self. Here alone does the full impact of those words, 'Not mine, but thy will be done', strike home. We know what the will of God is for the health and welfare of his creatures. We know what the will of God is for the unity of spirit that can bind creature and Creator into effective and power-filled relationship. But we also know the nature of the self-surrender that must be involved before that will can be realized. How utterly absurd it would have been for Jesus in the Garden of Gethsemane to have prayed as some exponents of merely psychological prayer would have suggested. To have said repeatedly, 'Gracious God, a cross has no place in my life,' would have moved him away from the basic choice that had to be made. But what he said was, 'In the face of my own personal desire, I still want to know the ultimate will and do it.' And this he prayed in anguish of spirit until his mind was clear. This kind of complete self-giving brings about the complete release of power within the being, both to do and to endure. The great deterrent to living with this kind of faith is fear of the power of the faith, and an unwillingness to let such faith dominate and

control life. Yet when the faith is complete the power becomes complete. Pilate with all his authority stood empty-handed and embarrassed before a faith that took the worst he had to offer and made of it a symbol of the triumph of the human spirit over external forms of power.

In our efforts to understand the power of a faith that can release life from its small and false limitations, we have to move beyond the devices that talk glibly to the lower levels of consciousness as if they were all of life. We need rather the mastery of self that can speak to all levels of being with a full realization of the nature of and power of the discipline that can at the same time constrain and release the freedom of choice as the ultimate of truths, for then alone do we understand what is meant by the words, 'and ye shall know the truth and the truth shall make you free'.

12

Restorative Processes at Work

Our lives are dynamic. No two days are alike. There is a continual coming and going, rising and falling, finding and losing. So it is that we need the powers of a faith that restores.

To have something and lose it is quite different from never having had it at all. Our conscious attitudes are different, and the feelings associated with them are different.

To have a nebulous, uncertain consciousness of need is quite different from being clearly aware of a condition that did exist and has been lost awhile, and which we would bring back again. For experience is a dimension of living, and consciously recorded and recalled living has a special reality for each individual. It is a part of life, and it varies from other parts of life as an experienced event differs from an imagined event.

If, for instance, a person was contemplating a trip to the Grand Canyon, he would project thoughts and feelings as his imagination worked in anticipation. His imagination would be built on descriptions, pictures and the reactions he might have to the experiences of others. Depending upon the quality of his imagination and the source material it had to feed upon, he would develop a picture of the Grand Canyon that would serve as a preconditioning for the real experience.

When he actually visited the Grand Canyon, his anticipation would be modified to fit the realities of his own experience. His sharpness of colour, his sense of depth and distance, his feelings of awe and wonder would then be readjusted to fit the real event

in his life that occurred when his own sensory equipment encountered the Grand Canyon.

If on a winter's evening a few months later he shows pictures of the Canyon to friends, he does so with a sense of the reality of the Canyon, which was built upon his imagination and his anticipation. The recollection, the restored picture, has a different quality about it from the picture projected in imagination. Another dimension of reality has been added by his own experience.

So it is when we deal with the faith that restores. We work with an experience. Sometimes it may be the experience of health that may have been casually taken for granted until it was lost, and then there is a deep need and desperate desire to have it restored. It may be a matter of inner security which has been an experience of the past and now does not exist, but would be recaptured in its original state or its current equivalent. Or it might be a life-sustaining faith that once was known and now seems to have evaporated from life, but would be restored if possible.

Because we are dealing with something that has been a part of the conscious mental processes, we are not so much concerned with the innate or the super-conscious, though it is important for us to realize that no experience is ever separated from the total response of the personality. This we recognize, but as a matter of convenience we are centring our thought upon those processes of conscious and deliberate mental activity which have as their purpose a restoration of a state of being that was but is not.

The process of re-experiencing

The processes of re-experiencing are varied and complicated. Much of what is involved in psychoanalytic procedure is the releasing of accumulated emotional energy in deeper levels of consciousness by the process of cathexis, a bringing to the conscious level of the submerged source of the accumulated emotion. I shall make no effort to deal with that sort of a process

in this chapter. I am dealing primarily with the data of memory and imagination as they can be used to activate and strengthen a state of mind and being that has existed, and is desired again.

Two basic problems engage us. One is that recollection is never complete, and the other is that the recalling person is never the same person who had the original experience or state of being. Recollection is partial and faulty, and influenced by emotions, and personality is a continuum always being modified by current experience.

McKeller says,

No memory image is a complete and accurate reproduction of a conceptual experience. The word 'image' is itself a little misleading in this respect, since visual images tend to be creative rather than accurate in any photographic sense, and the same applies to images of the other sense modes. . . No imagination image can occur that is not composed of elements derived from actual perceptual experiences; thus the differences between these and memory images is one of degree and not absolute. To understand imaginative thought it is necessary also to take account of the fact that we can have memory images of the products of other people's imaginings. We can learn about non-existent things by reading or seeing pictures of them.

The processes of recollection or re-experiencing, then, are complicated, involve an integrating of the total sensory response of the individual, and at the same time can be aided by the personality and experience of another. It is at this point that the counsellor or therapist may be of use in the process of re-experiencing.

One of the difficulties of convalescence for some persons is that they tend to become emotionally oriented about the experience of illness and its emotional benefits for them, and forget the state of health that once existed and needs to be recalled.

With others the onset of illness creates a state of mind and emotion that makes it hard to think in terms of health, and the

latent desire needs to be cultivated. Retarded physical function is apt to create states of depression that make direct re-experiencing difficult.

To re-establish the image of health and wholeness in the mind and emotion of the sick person is often an important part of the process of recovery. Sometimes a physician will say to the pastor, 'My patient does not seem to have much will to live. If you could say something to him to help change his attitude I am sure it would help his recovery.' In practical terms, this is a testimony to the importance of the faith that restores.

Sometimes the process of re-experiencing does not involve illness as much as it does a state of emotional security. When a boat is caught in a storm it is slight solace to try to recall that the number of calm days in proportion to the number of stormy ones is about six to one. The reality of the crisis is such that it tends to blot out all of the other circumstances of life. It is then that the amount of lead in the keel becomes the important factor for riding out the storm and keeping upright. The more stability that can be built up below the surface of life, the better set the individual is for the stormy sequences.

However, when a ship is caught in a gale, the situation seems precarious, and there is no time for criticizing the builder for failing to lead the keel properly. Then is a time for trimming sails, battening down the hatches, throwing out the sea anchor and just riding it out. Here the process of re-experiencing can be valuable, for the ability to meet storms gives assurance as one faces other crises that may come. Life at its best must face some crises, and the ability of the person to gain assurance from the past can be supplemented by his ability to learn from others even during the crisis experience. Here again the processes of counselling and therapy tend to be stabilizing influences in crises, so that one does not lose sight of the ultimate goals of life even when the going is difficult.

Sometimes the need for re-experiencing has to do with faith itself. John Wesley recorded in his *Journal* that when he felt his faith weakening he would preach a sermon on faith. In his effort to stimulate faith in the minds and emotions of others he found

a new assurance within himself, and this clarified his thinking and cleared up his confusion of emotion.

The conscious process of 'giving ourselves a good talking to' may often be all that is needed to move us beyond self-pity and easy acceptance of defeat. Our capacity for recall, and the creative imagination that can tie past experience to present conditions, can be a health-giving, life-restoring process. Add to this the assistance we can get from understanding and skilful counsellors, and we have a way of recapturing the faith that restores.

Achieving intro-psychic balance

Last night when I went to bed I was wondering how I should start this section on achieving intro-psychic balance. During the night, I received help from an unexpected source. In the little studio in the woods of a Vermont mountain-side where I write and think, I have had as house-guests this summer a family of field mice. They are such gracious and attractive little creatures that I have not had the heart to disturb them in their all-absorbing family life. While we have shown an interest in each other, it has been casual. I have let them alone, and apart from their habit of noisy eating in the middle of the night, they have not bothered me.

In the early hours of this morning I was startled in my sleep by a light thump upon my chest. My first impulse was to take some form of defensive or aggressive action against this unknown force that had awakened me. Then as sober consciousness returned I eliminated many of the possibilities and narrowed the unknown down considerably. I quietly reached for the light, and there sitting on my chest was a little mouse about two inches long, allowing an inch for tail. It was blinking its big eyes in the unaccustomed light. It looked as if it were trying to say, 'I meant no offence. I just lost my footing on that irregular shelf of books you have up there. I am young and haven't had much experience with such things, but give me another chance and I will try to do better next time.' So I put

the little mouse on a window ledge close to its nest, and started to think about what had happened during the few moments that had elapsed.

When an unknown, unaccustomed or unpleasant circumstance develops there is an inclination to respond with instinctive action that in most instances involves fright or flight, aggressive or defensive action against the unknown force that is assumed to be unfriendly. If and when the processes of reasoned judgment are allowed to go to work, the circumstances are evaluated more objectively and the appropriate action then can be taken without resorting to unnecessary defence or unreasoned aggression. The intruding forces are then accepted as friendly, even though they may have a minor amount of nuisance value connected to them. Reasonably friendly action can then be taken without interpersonal injury or intro-psychic complications.

Loss of intro-psychic balance is so often the product of a defensive or aggressive response to external circumstances that are not known or understood. The spontaneous action brings an equally spontaneous reaction, and the life-complicating experience ensues. Often the circumstance can be managed effectively with understanding of the cause, and a reduction of the emotional content of the situation. A basic faith in the essential friendliness of nature and human nature can help to curtail the instinctive reactions of fear.

Achieving emotional balance

The conscious re-education of the point of view is one of the important ways of reducing the negative emotional content of any given situation. Much of what is done in pastoral counselling is a re-education of the feelings so that they become comfortable with the intellectual insights that can be given. In and of itself, intellectual insight is often not enough to right a distress-creating situation. Often the person knows what should be done, but he does not have the feelings to stimulate the action.

Generally speaking, the re-establishing of balance in the

emotional ramparts of life grows from two techniques that the pastor may employ, either exclusive of each other or together. They are a supportive relationship and a process of clarification. Usually the supportive relationship is employed until the counsellor is sure that there is emotional strength enough to warrant the added stress of self-examination and behaviour change.

Let me illustrate this. Mrs L rang the bell at the pastor's study door at six a.m. When admitted she said she could not wait until morning. She didn't know where to turn, so had come to the pastor. Her son had called from three thousand miles away where he was serving with the Navy to say he had been arrested and was in jail and needed a hundred dollars for bail. Would she send it at once? She had not slept the rest of the night, did not know what to do, and was worried sick inside. The pastor did four things. First he listened to the whole story with sympathy and understanding of Mrs L's emotions. Then he told her she had done right to come to him and that she should try to relax as much as possible until they had all of the facts of the case. He explained something of the usual relation of civil and military law enforcement agencies, and the ways in which they correlate activities, and that until she had all the facts it was unwise to become overly excited and distressed. Then he said he would call the chaplain of the base as soon as the change in time belts warranted. Then he suggested that if she were willing they might wisely seek guidance in prayer. They did, and he indicated the need for divine guidance and calm wisdom in meeting life's problems. He told her he would call her as soon as he had word from the chaplain. A few hours later, when he talked with the chaplain, he found that the boy had already been released, no charges were being made, that youthful boisterousness had been complained of as a breach of the peace but that the light of day had changed dispositions and nothing would develop. The mother was greatly relieved and a sorely disturbed emotional state was restored to balance by a practical application of a faith in prayer and the instrumental-

ities of the pastoral function. Here a supportive relationship became the basis for the faith that restores emotional balance.

Often it is not as simple as that, and requires more time, more emotional energy, and more skill in a process of clarification. Unlike the supportive method, re-education aims to induce in the client an understanding of himself and his problem so that he may be better able to accept himself, together with his social milieu.

Otto C came to his pastor complaining about his wife and saying something would have to be done about her or he couldn't go on as things were. The pastor knew the family. The wife was competent and better educated than Otto C. They had three children ranging in ages from two to ten. Otto was a big, hard-working plumber whose views of life and especially home life were simple, direct and strongly flavoured by the German background and large family from which he had come. At first he was allowed to blow off steam. As he talked it was obvious his complaints were mostly about child-rearing methods. During a period of several weeks and many hours, Otto was led to consider the nature of a child's personality, the meaning of behaviour, the mother's role and the father's role with children. Comparisons were made between the American home and the German home. No judgments were made, and nothing was said about right and wrong ways to do things. Otto became very much interested in what to him was an entirely new idea. He looked at himself and some of the things he did with almost an amused understanding. Again and again he would say, 'What do you know about that!' or 'Who would have thought it?', as he gained insight about his own way of doing things. Especially as he compared his efforts to quell the exuberance of his family about the table at meal time, he was appalled to find that he was doing exactly as his father had always done in making the children eat in silence. But his father had had more success. He was frustrated because he could not succeed and yet he never liked the way his father had done things. A gradual change came over his behaviour as he began to see and understand about himself. After a while he said he didn't think he would

need to come any more because things had worked out. His wife wrote the pastor a thank you note in which she said the most important thing that had happened was that they were now able to talk things over and decide together what was a sensible way of doing things. This had eliminated the thunder and lightning in their family life.

Here was a process of restoring emotional balance to a situation through the conscious processes of insight and the related modifications of behaviour. The problems of attitude were met, not with a frontal attack, but as if all emotions have a meaning if the meaning can be explored and revealed to the full consciousness.

Achieving physical wholeness

At the Mayo Clinic there has been made a useful correlation of certain types of emotional states and the physical symptoms that tend to accompany them. Irritable persons develop skin irritations. Angry people develop the symptoms of constrictive rage reactions. Unhappy people develop congestion of the respiratory tract as if they were about to cry but couldn't. Fearful people develop chronic symptoms of the temporary fear-releasing mechanisms, such as a spastic colon. The major emotions have their major physical expressions. The physical restoration of normal, healthful living quite naturally then implies some sort of action to deal with the underlying emotions. This employs the faith which restores right feelings.

The conscious attitude that we have toward a physical condition certainly has a bearing upon that condition. Perhaps this has nowhere been better shown than in the Reed method of natural childbirth. Here thoughts and feelings are dealt with at the conscious level. Early in the pregnancy the expectant mothers meet together in classes where the processes of gestation are explained. False ideas of the past are examined. The relation of the pains of childbirth to the racial punishment of evil are explained, and cast away. The wonders and the privileges of childbirth are emphasized. The processes by which the actual

birth takes place are described and illustrated by pictures. A phonographic record of the conversation between a mother and a physician during a delivery is played. An anticipation of the wonderful event is created, rather than the fear of a frightening event. In order for the expectant mothers to be in the best condition possible for the important event, physical training is done in classes and alone. Exercises to prepare special muscles for their work are encouraged. As athletes in training for a special event, so the mothers are conditioned in body, mind and spirit for the important event that will engage them. The process of conditioning mind, emotion and physique is continued until the day of delivery. Nothing is to remain unfamiliar, unreasonable or frightening. All is directed toward reasonable interpretation, calm and quiet understanding, and a joyful expectancy. As a result, the being is prepared for the event. The pains that are a result of fear-constricted muscles are eliminated, and the full cooperation of an understanding and accepting person engages in a wonderful, life-producing process. The benefits to mother and child are clearly demonstrable.

Here is a faith that restores the person to right relations with reality, rather than a fearful relationship with falsehood. So often in the restoring of health and wholeness, the conscious understanding of what is taking place can be useful. The doctor who invites the cooperation of the patient by a careful preparation of the patient and a cooperative approach to the patient reduces the fear and the mystery of disease, and stimulates the health-producing response of the organism.

The mind that can be focused in the creative and restorative processes in nature that bring health back to the being becomes an ally in the healing process. So the fever is not an enemy but an evidence of the vigour with which the body fights infection. The aches and the pains that are sometimes experienced are the adjustments of tissue to the new surges of life. Even those conditions we least expect to be healthful may well be. When a badly wounded soldier was brought into the emergency dressing station in World War I and it was found that maggots were already at work on the gangrenous tissue, revulsion was felt,

but a young doctor ordered the dressing changed but the maggots left undisturbed. The little creatures consumed the poison but did not touch the living tissue. The young doctor was invited to join the staff of Johns Hopkins to breed sterile maggots for therapeutic purposes, and what at first appeared to be loathsome was life-restoring. So the earth yields up the ingredients of terramyacine. The sources of life-restoring health are more abundant than we often know. It is important for the restoration of health to our bodies to realize that we are not carrying on a lonely fight against great odds, but that we are cooperating with the whole pulse of nature in its efforts to release and restore life to its full measure of perfection, for the image of God upon matter is the image of perfection. To restore the perfect image to the life of body, mind and spirit is not an isolated and isolating struggle but rather the important movement in which all of nature and nature's God unite.

The faith that restores life makes abundant use of the power of the mind to understand and direct its energy towards wholeness of being. This can be done by recall, by achieving balanced understanding, and by bringing a perceptive mind into active cooperation with a body that has upon it the marks of nature's wisdom. A major function of the religious consciousness is the stimulating and directing of this kind of mental competence in dealing with the experience of life.

13

New Insight on Faith as a Life Force

We have looked at what an innate faith can do to release the resources of life.

We have looked at what the consciously directed mind can do to help the restorative processes.

Let us now look at that something extra that can be at work in life to bring faith to its finest fulfilment. This something comes from beyond the conscious self. The Psalmist put it in simple form when he said, 'I would have fainted, but for the Lord.' When we have done all we know, there is still an important power at work.

To redeem means to take the potential value and make it actual. A person with trading stamps takes them to the trading centre and redeems the stamps by turning their potential into an actual and walks home with the actual under his arm.

In religious terms the process of redemption applies to the whole of life. 'God so loved that he gave' to redeem life, to turn its spiritual potential into a spiritual actual. How does this come about?

When potential values become actual

Perhaps the greatest of all of the mysteries that is to be plumbed by the human mind is the mystery of the Holy Spirit. We cannot begin to evaluate the potential value or power of a human being unless we make an effort to assay our actual value as a created

being. Our created value always seems to be far and away above any of those means that men employ for establishing worth. If the redemptive process is to help man achieve his actual worth, some way must be established at least to approach that realm of value. It is certainly not achieved by any of the standards of chemical, physical, or mechanistic valuation of which we know anything. If we interpret the Holy Spirit as that bond of understanding relationship and mutual acceptance that existed between Jesus and God, as some of the mediaeval mystics did, then we can perhaps begin to make this nebulous idea more specific and relevant for our purposes.

In speaking of that basic pull of life which, like its equivalent in the law of gravity, brings all things into their proper relationship with a divine principle, St Augustine said, 'My love is my weight'. In the Introduction to Boehme's *Three Dialogues of the Supersensual Life*, Bernard Holland writes,

> In a deep sense, the desire of the Spark of Life in the Soul to return to its Original Source is part of the longing desire of the universal Life for its own heart and centre. Of this longing, the universal attraction, striving against resistance, towards a universal centre, proved to govern the phenomenal or physical world, is but the outer sheath and visible working. . . Desire is everything in Nature; does everything. Heaven is Nature filled with divine Life attracted by Desire.[1]

Much the same idea expressed in different words comes from Eckhart.

> The best masters say that the love wherewith we love is the Holy Spirit. Some deny it. But this is always true: all those motives by which we are moved to love, in these is nothing else than the Holy Spirit.

In yet other words Ruysbroeck expresses the comparable idea.

> God wills that we should come forth from ourselves in this Eternal Light; that we should reunite ourselves in a super-

natural manner with that image which is our true Life, and that we should possess it with Him actively and fruitively in eternal blessedness . . . this giving forth of the contemplative is also in Love: for by fruitive love he overpasses his created being and finds and tastes the riches and delights that are God himself, and which He causes to pour forth without ceasing in the most secret chambers of the soul, at that place where it is most like unto the nobility of God.[2]

If these same ideas were to be expressed in modern psychological terms, we might say that the Holy Spirit is complete integration and direction of life by an all-consuming life-affirming, life-accepting, affective principle. The achieving of this state resolves aggressive feeling and action and life-crippling defence mechanisms, and frees all the innate, conscious and super-conscious energy of life for its full creative expression. In fact, much this sort of thing has been said by a psychiatrist who gives persons the alternative to 'Love or perish'. And socially oriented psychiatrists like Eric Fromm say quite frankly that the function of the psychiatrist is to free the life of the patient from his unreasonable restraint on love. It is a process of learning to love.

Whether it is in the mystical terminology of the religious mystic, or the psychological language of the contemporary student of personality, both express the same idea, that the actual value of the human spirit is realized only through the life-freeing act of learning to love with all levels of being in all relationships of life. The New Testament commandment that united these six points was simply put. 'Love God with heart and soul and mind and strength, and neighbour as self.' Here the premise of self-love is basic. However, the idea is not one of self-indulgence that leads to self-dissolution and self-destruction but of self-discipline that leads to self-realization and self-fulfilment. This capacity for self-acceptance and self-realization is the basic premise for any healthful social contact, and the neighbour here is conceived as anyone for whom there is a possibility of accepting response. These are both built on the

larger premise that the complete giving of self in a redeeming faith related to an all-consuming cosmic acceptance is basic to any capacity to love. To love God with all of one's being, body, soul, mind and strength, is to give conscious support to the action of the innate capacity to respond at the same time that a mystical awareness through the agency of the super-conscious mind is allowed freedom to bring to the self a transcendent experience of the more-than-self.

One of our difficulties in dealing effectively with the concept of God as love, which is so fruitful in the New Testament, is the paucity of verbal symbols for such feelings in our language. New Testament Greek can help us at this point.

The New Testament uses three Greek words to express the full meaning of love: *eros*, *phileo*, and *agape*. *Eros* we well know as the root of the word erotic, and its association is primarily with sensuousness. The word *phileo* relates more to the intellectual processes that express an open and accepting attitude and are used primarily in such words as philosophy, the love of knowledge or wisdom. The word *agape* carries with it the meaning of full self-giving and commitment. It is the word used in the phrase, 'God so loved that he gave.' It is the word that Jesus used in his interrogation of Peter, when the answer of Peter the first two times changed the word of the question into another word for the answer. The first two times Jesus asked, 'Peter, lovest thou me?' Peter used the word *phileo* in his answer, though Jesus used the word *agape* in his question. Only on the third repetition of the question did Peter respond with the word *agape*. Jesus wanted to know whether his commitment was merely an intellectual assent, or whether it carried with it the full measure of his loyalty and devotion.

In speaking of God as love, we are dealing with the full and complete commitment of being. Yet this is not an easily achieved form of existence. Kepler the astronomer wrote, 'My wish is that I may perceive God, whom I find everywhere in the external world, in like manner within and inside me.' The quest for knowledge through the senses is a simpler and more easily satisfied pursuit. The finding of the meaning of life comes not

by easy assent, but by a tortuous discipline that moves beyond the wisdom of the senses to a more all-encompassing wisdom that fulfils all that the senses have to contribute, and then completes it in a 'full, fine, careless rapture'.

We do not begin to contemplate the potential that can become actual in a human being until we approach it in such terms. But how can we move from the actual we envisage to the potential we desire?

A psychological process of relationship

In the nature of man there is brought together that which is and is becoming, the finite and the infinite, the material and the spiritual, the free and the determined, the self-conscious and the self-impelled. The process by which this conglomerate is brought into a spiritual unity completely responsive to a cosmic desire is not an easy matter to contemplate, let alone achieve.

In the processes of nature which produce this spiritual sensitivity there appear to be three levels at which the redemptive process is at work, the racial, the social and the personal.

In his biological studies, Sinnott of Yale sees the slow emergence of the qualities of spirit. Life ever moves from the less complicated toward the more complicated, and it is the more complicated forms of life that produce the specialized functions which give rise to the qualities of the spiritual life. All of nature seems to move in this direction.

Von Domarus, also of Yale, has projected an interpretation of anthropology, starting with the conflict between the tree apes and the ground apes, which moves toward a developing consciousness in man that makes it possible for him to deal wisely and well with more and more complicated life situations. In some stages this involves conflict and the use of brute force. At other stages it invites a mutual aid factor, and at still other levels it produces a spiritual awareness that makes it possible for men to respond to a cosmic plan and a nature within themselves that is life-valuing and life-fulfilling. Von Domarus calls this the emergence of the 'religious man'. So the long slow struggle of

racial history is not without its purpose. Struggling upwards, and sliding backwards, but learning and developing, man makes mistakes, pays the price and then moves on the slow, tortuous way toward his full realization of a spiritual nature.

The same sort of process is at work in the social or cultural group to bring a sense of value and worth to life. Certain groups seem to possess a destiny and national purpose that stimulate the activities by group practice and incentives to the individual to reach toward a messianic fulfilment or a state of Nirvana. Through its long history, the Jewish nation has kept clearly before the minds of its people the high dream towards which they could add their measure of fulfilment, if only by keeping the dream alive. This has led to a group life of deep religious devotion, with constancy in adversity and courage in facing new situations, which in turn has found expressions in the lives of individual members of the group who were inventive, creative in the arts and sciences, and most of all deeply perceptive in the awareness of the ultimate meaning and value of life itself. In India also there has been the type of group life that gave status to the Holy Man and encouraged the soarings of the religious spirit. This has led to a particularly fertile growth of psychological insight and super-conscious sensitivity, not only in theory but also in the methods that can be employed towards that type of self-realization. So we have in the disciplined understanding of Indian psychology and religion many of the insights that have only recently come into the stream of Western culture through the psychoanalytic disciplines.

While the race and the nation make their contributions to this kind of a redemptive process, the full realization of the meaning of life inevitably shows itself in the life of an individual. Religious literature is filled with the experiences of these persons who claim to have had the mystical illumination which has given to their lives its ultimate meaning. Here the processes of evaluation must be employed with great care, for, as the assayer of precious metals must be able to tell the difference between real gold and 'fool's gold', so we must be able to tell the difference in the experience which emanates from the subcon-

scious from the experience that comes through the agency of the super-conscious.

In psychoanalytic study the 'oral triad' is referred to as that state of mind and emotion which is produced by a regression to early experiences in the relation of the child and its mother. Under deep emotional stress there is an inclination of the personality to retreat to a condition where problems were effectively solved. When the child was distressed by hunger pains it cried, and the mother was immediately there to satisfy the needs with warmth, loving care and food 'divinely mingled, fit and good'. There was a feeling of omnipotence in the powerful control over the outer world which is probably never again felt in life. There is the satisfaction of food and drink, of comfort and sleep, and of a feeling of ineffable unity and power into which one sinks with complete trust. Many of the writings of those who claim the redemptive revelation repeat these three attitudes, and seem to imply that what has happened has been a re-experiencing of an early and satisfying emotional state which helps to relieve the current stress of life. Such experience is rooted in the subconscious mind of the individual who has the experience.

The redemptive experience that comes through the super-conscious level of being is much rarer, more difficult to attain, and usually a very costly event in the life of a person. The principle that all life is giving of life to others at cost to the self is one of the core principles which underly the doctrine of atonement. Just as the rare mathematical genius with little training and background is able to perform unbelievable feats of mental power in the field of figures, so the rare quality of mind of the religious genius achieves rare insight and understanding about the nature of life and its ultimate meaning. The certainty which he feels can be reality-tested in time, but those who are willing to do it are usually few and far between. It is easier to destroy the seer than to accept and adjust to his insight. So it is that often those who have borne the burden of spiritual illumination have suffered for it. But it is equally true that through them in time the benefits of such experience can be

passed on to others, so that many may benefit from the insights of the illuminated few. So in time, as reality has been tested and the fruits of the super-conscious insight have been made valid for life, the many share in the benefits and the general level of insight and understanding grows.

So the redemptive process is at work at various levels. As our bodies can travel at three speeds without incongruity as the body moves on the earth, and the earth moves on its axis and the earth continues to move about the sun, so the movement towards the realization of the fullest meaning for the spiritually conscious life is achieved at varying speeds at one and the same time by the race in its upward movement, by groups that are especially sensitive, and by the individuals who share the burden of the super-conscious illumination.

Science illuminates faith as a life force

A. Clutton Brock tries to write a prescription for the achieving of the spiritual consciousness. While it will not be normative for all individuals, it will elevate our sights so that we are focused on something more than a subconscious emotional reversion.

> For all spiritual experience, whether of art or of life, we need a self-surrender, a willing removal of obstructions in our own minds, a sacrifice of the obvious, of what is called common sense. We must forget what the ego habitually says to us, so that we may hear something else speak; we need to deny ourselves and follow. For spiritual experience is always surprising. . . Just as the man of science must give up his theories before facts, so we must rid ourselves of all the inhibitions of habit that seems to us wisdom, when spiritual experience offers itself to us. . . We must have the habit of scepticism about all the possessions of our own minds if we are to let truth happen to us; we must utterly rid ourselves of the desire to be proved right. . . To know yourself nothing, and then to find yourself charged with all the power of that to which you have yielded, that is the highest power man can

attain to. . . At the height of spiritual experience we are like the bandit who was imprisoned for years in a loathsome dungeon, until one day it occurred to him to open the door and walk out. . . And the self at one moment leads up to the self at another; and the whole universe at one moment leads up to the whole universe at another; and there is a oneness in both only seen at the height of spiritual experience. . . It is the bewilderment that has fallen away from spiritual experience and denied it, which turns the brain sick and makes men rush into blasphemy and savagery for relief. But all this is merely pathological, like those states of mind in which our identity seems to be divided and we are unreal to ourselves, since there is no self to be real to. . . So the only cure for nightmares of scepticism is spiritual experience. . . We can be at one, not with nature in the scientist's sense, but with that personal in it which we see in spiritual experience. We can become like the lilies of the field as Christ saw them; and, when we do, they will not be to us flowers in the hair of the fairy angel, but like ourselves, creatures and children of God.[3]

Here is the culmination of the artist's consciousness, not in terms of some structured symbol that he would make real to others, but as the realization of the ultimate of the fine arts which he does not have to symbolize for himself, for he experiences it, nor for others, for they do not know its meaning except as they experience it. So it is so much a part of life's finer feelings, that cannot be described but can be felt. Who would adequately express the meaning of a mother's love or a father's willing self-giving? Who would put into words the artist's vision or its expression in a masterpiece? In each instance a verbal description is but a starting-point for the larger realization. So the super-conscious mental activity, at work in man, cannot be reduced to a lower form without losing that which is its distinctive quality. But the way can be pointed, the knowledge of the power can be confirmed, and the questing soul can be invited to 'Wait patiently for him'.

Self-actualization as a way to wholeness

We come now to a paradox, and a paradox that we must resolve, or much that we have said about faith will stand meaningless and unavailing. How can there be an invasion of the self by the beyond self? If the Kingdom of God is within, what is there without that adds to the inner kingdom? In what sense can we speak of a unity between creature and creator if one is without and one is within?

First, we must realize that the unity is a process and not a state of being. If I hold a sunflower seed in my hand, and say, 'Here is all that is needed to produce a magnificent flower that will follow the light of the sun throughout the day,' you may say 'Yes, but. . .' The seed has all of the qualities of pattern, design, built-in wisdom and latent energy, waiting to be directed towards its goal of self-fulfilment. But unless it is free to respond, it will remain dormant, and the life that is in it may fade away with time. The potential of the sunflower seed becomes actual when its inner kingdom is set free to be what it was meant to be, and this can only happen when it is creatively related to the beyond-self. The individuality, the uniqueness, the unrealized power of the seed comes to life when it is united with the beyond-self that is above and below. There is the chemistry of the earth that goes to work to stimulate growth. There is the radiation of the sun that goes to work to stimulate growth. There is the moisture from earth and sky that goes to work to stimulate growth. The pattern of the seed is realized only in a working relationship with that which is beyond itself.

When Jesus held a grain of mustard in his hand and said, 'Except ye have faith like a grain of mustard. . .', he was not inviting his listeners to accept a small amount of faith. A mustard seed is small, but there are no dimensions to measure the nature of its faith. A mustard seed is committed without reservation to the design and pattern that is within it. It never says to itself, 'I resent my status, and therefore I will rebel and become a poppy seed instead.' Its acceptance of itself and its design is at no point complicated by the burdensome privileges

of freedom of choice. Because it is not free, it is completely committed to its purpose. Jesus looked at men and asked them to achieve the same measure of commitment to a pattern and design built into themselves as a part of their endowment when they were made in the image of God. All that is needed to fulfil that purpose is present in the design and pattern of the human soul. All of the unrealized possibilities are there waiting for the moment when they will be united with that below and that above which can set them free from their misuse of freedom and bring them to that tremendous power of self-realization that turns a seed to a great flower, or a human soul to a reservoir flowing rich with the power of God that waits to be released through them. There is no contradiction of terms. There is no violation of purpose. The inner kingdom can become all it was intended to be only when it chooses to respond to its spiritual equivalent of sunlight, chemistry and moisture. Interestingly enough, the New Testament symbols of the nature of God are not bound up with a state of being as much as they are with a process of power. The words used are Light, Love, Power and Spirit.

Raynor C. Johnson, Master of Queen's College, Melbourne, has for years been a professor of physics. Along with that he has studied the findings of psychical research and the nature of the mystical experience. In them he finds not so much a regression to the lower forms of consciousness, but rather a growing edge of the unrealized potential of the human mind and spirit. Using the insight of modern physics he looks into the microcosm, the infinitesimal world of the atom, and finds that 'none of our mental concepts – colour, position, shape, sound resistance to touch, etc. – apply here. Indeed Space and Time which seem to dominate our familiar world are quite elusive in the microcosm.'[4] We are so built that our sensory equipment can only be aware of a limited range of reality. This is markedly true of those areas of penetration which modern physics has revealed to us in recent decades. But this is equally true of the macrocosm, the majestic realm where the astronomer's measurements assume a magnitude that makes our finite minds equally far from

home. If our sensory equipment is conceived to place boundaries on our imaginations, we are like the mustard seed that wants to deny its function. But if the varied equipment and insight that comes to us from our sensory equipment as it is amplified by the instruments of science becomes the fertile ground for our imaginations, and the sense of our purpose in creation becomes the sunlight to stimulate our growth, the grandeur of the nature of a human being is beyond conceiving.

Human beings with their self-consciousness and God-consciousness stand in a strategic position between the cell and the celestial. Humans alone are patterned and designed to be aware of a cosmic relationship. Humans alone can deny God's purpose and deny his pattern. He can refuse to accept the power resources that can help him develop his embryo mind and spirit to the place where it is not slave of what it perceives, but uses its perception to free its imagination so that it may soar. Two creatures of nature illustrate the choice that may be made. In the long processes of evolution the turtle has accepted the demands for a defensive approach to life and has boxed itself in. It has traded many of the finer qualities of existence for a protection that it has drawn securely around itself. The bird, on the other hand, was once a reptile, but it sought the higher reaches, and gradually modified its nature until it could soar. So man, throughout the long slow processes of emergence, has developed a capacity to soar. He is free to limit it, deny it or even to destroy it. Or he can use the special endowment of his consciousness to build a bridge of understanding and acceptance between the power of the microcosm and the macrocosm, and use both for the glory of that design that is in him, to fulfil his nature as a being made in the image of God, sharing his creative imagination and using the latent power that is his.

Scientists now say that the universe is more like a great thought than a great thing. It is the Dean of the School of Science at MIT who says,

We must grow with our universe. It is turning out to be more marvellous than man has ever dreamed, more beautiful while

more complex, fuller of that which we consider good than philosophers of earlier days could care to expect. Man's new directions of thought are filled with meaning for the coming races of mankind, and will lead him into new fields of awareness, new challenges of attainment, and new realizations of human destiny. . . The distilled spiritual wisdom of humanity coincides closely with what science reveals in nature.[5]

And so we would grow, as part of a great process, not in the strange paradox of denial of our nature, but in that realization that nourishes the inner kingdom with all that is made available for its development. There is achieved a unity that takes all that man is and helps him to use it to achieve all that he can become.

This, then, becomes the faith of the mustard seed, that takes the nature of man and uses all the resources of creation to bring it to its fullest self-realization. In the redemptive process by which the potential becomes actual, and the within-self is supported by the beyond-self, the power of a personality may be at work, as when Jesus saw the power of Peter into realization, or in a vision whereby the power of Paul was made available for fulfilment, or in the less dramatic but equally important growth where a man opens his mind and spirit to the divine plan in him, and grows toward its fulfilment.

In summary, we have looked at faith, not as a body of belief, however valid and important for life that may be, but as a quality of being. We have tried to describe this quality of being as it works in all levels of life, body, mind and spirit. We have tried to show that it is a living quality that does things to life at all levels of being. Only as we begin to think of faith in these broader terms will we begin to understand what are some of the varied possibilities at work in the restoring of life to wholeness through the power of faith. Only then can we begin to understand the importance of prayer as it can be employed as an instrument for the developing of the qualities of mind and spirit that make faith a life-fulfilling quality of being.

14

Spiritual Therapy Rediscovered

In order to understand the possibilities of meditation as a dynamic force in life, we must do as we have tried to do with faith – redefine it not in terms of a traditional structure of beliefs that one has about life, but rather as a force that is at work in life. So meditation becomes not something that is said or done. It is rather a way of being, a disciplined process of thought that seeks to bring life into accord with its highest purpose. So it is not something you do but is something you are.

This may seem confusing after so much of the teaching we have had in the past about what you do when you pray. But we must move beyond our confusion, and the misinformation that we have inherited from those who meant well but understood little, so that we can begin to inherit that kingdom which we have so often prayed might come upon the earth.

Fortunately this idea of prayer has deep roots in the New Testament. We are admonished to pray without ceasing. This, of course, can only be realistic if we are dealing with a way of life rather than one of its minor activities. We are told to pray for one another so that the healing process may take place. We are led to believe that there are strict prerequisites for effective prayer, for it is the fervent prayer of the righteous man that avails. We have demonstrated the special moods and the special powers of prayer where circumstance is demanding. We have evidence that the disciples felt the uniqueness of Jesus was found more in his understanding of prayer than any other aspect of life, for it alone invited their request for special instruction.

That this type of prayer was a strenuous discipline is evidenced by the anguished encounter of man with destiny that led Jesus to sweat blood.

Let any one be quickly disavowed if he thinks the kind of prayer we are thinking about is any trivial process whereby a selfish individual seeks to work some magical power to manipulate external circumstances to satisfy some personal desire. Prayer as we think of it does not project either an anthropomorphic picture of a cosmic errand boy or even the benign figure of a celestial Santa Claus who bends his ear to the petitions for things or services.

Rather, it is a determined effort to bring the self into accord with cosmic purposes. Often this involves a heroic restraint upon the self and a constraint upon the self-will, so that the larger will that is seeking to express itself through the prayer may be realized.

This approach to prayer is finding support from those who are not strictly within the field of professional religious interpretation. They recognize that this kind of prayer is specialized thinking, and thinking is a life-modifying type of experience. So the self is engaged with the beyond-self in an encounter that bears fruit in the symptoms of changed living, a new sense of health and wholeness.

Meditation a way to perspective

Jesus often went apart into a quiet place for meditation and contemplation. Something happens to life through this kind of a process. Alexis Carrel describes it thus:

> Man integrates himself by meditation, just as by action. But he should not be content with contemplating the beauty of the ocean, of the mountains, and of the clouds, the masterpieces of the artists and the poets, the majestic constructions of philosophical thought, the mathematical formulas which express natural laws. He must also be the soul which strives to attain a moral ideal, searches for light in the darkness of

this world, marches forward along the mystic way, and renounces itself in order to apprehend the invisible substratum of the universe. . . Prayer should be understood, not as a mere mechanical recitation of formulas, but as a mystical elevation, an absorption of consciousness in the contemplation of a principle both permeating and transcending our world.[1]

The kind of prayer that is here described moves at three levels. It produces effects upon the person of the one who prays, for though it involves more than psychological laws, it starts from them. The meditating person in his contemplation not only of beauty but of the sources of beauty changes the focus of his life so that instead of the discordant he views the harmonious; instead of the disruptive, he sees that which integrates. Thus the power of suggestion directs him away from the more morbid preoccupations, and helps him to dwell on those things that are more pleasant, rewarding and inspiring. While prayer is much more than suggestion, its total impact upon life is to saturate it with life-enriching suggestion.

It also involves communion with the beyond-self. This communion may be varied by mood and content. It may be silent adoration, it may be intercession. It certainly includes great affirmation, but not merely as suggestion, for the processes of suggestion may end with the affirmations. This level of prayer calls forth the discipline of dedication, purification, the limitation of self-will and the laying hold of the power to accomplish these things through the active mental and spiritual relationship of creature and Creator.

The third level of prayer is a spiritual achievement built on the other two. It is as much more than communication as communication is more than suggestion. It is the achievement of a mystical unity with divine purpose and power so that all of the resources of being are at the disposal of the beyond-self, and in this complete self-giving is realized the full possibility of the self as a spirit dominated being. Comparable to the beatific

vision, this stage of prayer comes only to those who prepare for it and are found worthy.

Each of these levels of prayer involves a withdrawal, not necessarily physical. Rather it involves the determined effort to move away from the attitudes, values and preoccupations that normally engage us so that we can become aware of and fulfil a higher destiny.

A historical note is important here. Traditionally in the life of the church those who went apart for fasting and self-discipline did so as if their bodies were their enemies. They tortured and abused their physical being. Our sense of being as a living unity would not discount or injure the body, but would rather have it share all of the benefits of fulfilment. So withdrawal would be an act of disciplined renewal for body, mind and spirit. The physical benefits of such a process of prayer could not but benefit the total functioning of the body, for it would share the processes of renewal and regeneration. For surely the body is the temple of the living God.

Meditation as return

'In returning and in rest shall ye be saved. In quietness and in confidence shall be your strength.' The importance of return has long been recognized. Too often in history those who have set themselves to the tasks of prayer have retreated into a world of their own and have become lost in their own reveries of spirit. They have lost that social bond that could keep their prayer life actively bound up with the needs and concerns of their day. They developed a power and a capacity, but failed to make it significant for the life of their time because it remained largely potential and not actual.

An important part of the Wesleyan revival movement that is seldom mentioned was the activities of the 'bands'. Different from the classes which met for study and the societies which brought together the classes in public worship, the 'bands' were small groups limited to seven or eight who came together for meditation, self-examination and prayer. Employing many of

the insights of the small group therapy approach they exerted a great influence in the lives of their members. They were not withdrawn or separated, but played a major part in giving goals and incentives to English society that helped to prevent the kind of reaction against industrial breakdown that might have been expressed through the English equivalent of the French Revolution.

One of the important reformation movements of our day is taking place quietly but powerfully among those thousands of small groups who are seriously studying the methods and processes of prayer. Their lives are being modified, and their influence through intercession is reaching out. Aware of the great force, they are trying to learn to be worthy of it. Unsophisticated in social context, they are through discipline and directed effort becoming the elite of the spirit. As Carrel mentions, 'But the simple seem to feel God as easily as the heat of the sun or the kindness of a friend.' Bound by no other purpose than to develop the life of the spirit, the members of these small groups are finding the meaning of all of life. And they are unconsciously relating it to the total health of their own beings just as they tend to purify themselves as they engage in the activities of praying for another.

Carrel as a physician gives interesting interpretations of the mood and attitude of this kind of life changing prayer. He says,

Certain spiritual activities may cause anatomical as well as functional modifications of the tissues and the organs. These organic phenomena are observed in various circumstances, among them being the state of prayer. . . The prayer that is followed by organic effects is of a special nature. First, it is entirely disinterested. Man offers himself to God. He stands before him like the canvas before the painter or the marble before the sculptor. At the same time, he asks for his Grace, exposes his needs and those of his brothers in suffering. Generally, the patient who is cured is not praying for himself. But for another. Such a type of prayer demands complete renunciation – that is, a higher form of asceticism. The

modest, the ignorant, and the poor are more capable of this self-denial than the rich and the intellectual. When it possesses such characteristics, prayer may set in motion a strange phenomenon, the miracle.[2]

The return we mean is the deliberate effort to keep the processes of prayer related to the rest of life. Then, their effects cannot be unrelated to the deep emotions and the physical manifestations of these emotions in the state of being we know as health.

Meditation as contemplation

So much has been written about prayer as contemplation that we may easily be confused. We may get the idea that it is a way of life where like the Yogi one sits for hours contemplating his own navel. Or we may think it is a type of mental exercise which is engaged in by persons who go through the same rituals as all other persons and come out with the same kinds of results. So the formulas of meditation may emphasize the employing of self and the relating of the emptied self to sources of power and insight beyond the self.

It is important to realize that contemplation is never separated from all that the person is and does. All we have been able to learn about the unconscious makes us increasingly aware of the fact that it is difficult for a person to get away from himself. Even the most pure and the most adept at contemplation have to deal with this fact of their own identity and their peculiar individuality.

Gerald Heard reminds us that contemplation may in its quiet detachment draw from the deep wells of the spirit, but like an artesian well, the water must pass through the numerous strata of rock before it reaches the surface. The contamination of the springs of the spirit is always a possibility, and the quest for pure motives and worthy insight must always be guarded against the intrusions of aggressive feelings and contaminating thoughts. So contemplation is never an easy and assured

approach to spiritual enlightenment. It is a process that demands the best insight and understanding of the self and others
to guide its progress.

For this reason, contemplation in a group may be a useful
discipline. One evening a group of young women began to talk
about the ways in which anger interfered with effective prayer.
Before long they were dealing with such subjects as the disguises
their anger wore, the ways in which anger complicated the
expression of their love towards their children, what happened
when they approached a new situation with angry feelings, and
how they could understand the deep roots of anger so that they
could better control it. Having been together as a group for
quite a long time they felt free to express their thoughts and
feelings without restraint. There was confession not as abject
self-abnegation, but rather as one holding himself up before a
light to look at something new about his being. There was an
employing of psychological understanding that dealt with the
causes of anger deep in life, and the obligations upon adults to
keep from doing to a new generation what had been done to
them. Here was creative contemplation that grew from a
cross-fertilization of thought.

So often we have been led to believe that contemplation is
limited to some sort of a vapid sitting before a sea or a mountain
to think the thoughts one traditionally thinks in such places.
Far from it. Contemplation involves the taking of time to look
carefully into the meaning and purpose of life, especially as it
deals with the life of the spirit. It calls for honest, muscular
thinking. Someone may well employ the kind of criticism that
comes from the group experience. It is far from being an escape
into unreality, for it seeks to deal with what is real in the
experience of life, in the self and in others.

This kind of searching self-exploration may break loose some
of the defences and devices of escape that keep us from facing
life, and sometimes we will stumble on the fact that those types
of behaviour that we have cherished because of their
attention-getting, sympathy-creating symptoms are parts of
indefensible behaviour patterns that we employ to get around

some unpleasant aspects of the reality of living. Such contemplation, then, may have a real bearing on our health and wholeness of being.

Meditation as subjective-objective bridge

The complicated processes of consciousness make it difficult to tell the difference between the objectively real and the subjectively real. This may profoundly affect the mental and spiritual mechanisms that have to do with cause-effect relationships. Modern science tends to minimize the distinctions between the organic and the inorganic, the particle and the wave, the timely and the timeless, the measured and the measureless. In the physical sciences the old forms of measurement no longer serve a purpose, for that which was traditionally material is now characterized more by its spiritual qualities of energy and motion. So also it appears to be with the traditional distinctions between the subjective and the objective. More than we realize, they share a mystical unity, and one cannot understand one without dealing with the other. But it is not easy to build a bridge of consciousness between the two so that they can be dealt with as a living unity.

Here again Carrel does suggestive thinking for us. He writes,

Each state of consciousness probably has a corresponding organic expression. Emotions, as is well known, determine the dilation or the contraction of the small arteries, through the vasomotor nerves. They are, therefore, accompanied by changes in the circulation of the blood in tissues and organs. Pleasure causes the skin of the face to flush. Anger and fear turn it white. In certain individuals, bad news may bring about a spasm of the coronary arteries, anaemia of the heart, and sudden death. The affective states act on all the glands by increasing or decreasing their circulation. They stimulate or stop their secretions, or modify their chemical constitution... An emotion may set in action complex mechanisms... Thus, envy, hate, fear, when these sentiments

are habitual, are capable of starting organic changes and genuine diseases. Moral suffering profoundly disturbs health. . . Thought can generate organic lesions. . . In a like manner, those who keep the peace in their inner self in the midst of the tumult of the modern city are immune from nervous and organic disorders.[3]

Prayer as a specialized state of consciousness moves the being beyond the usual considerations of real or unreal, conscious or unconscious, organic or inorganic, subjective or objective, to the place where he is dealing with the totality of his being at one and the same time in a way that produces a sensitivity to the whole. As George Russell put it simply, 'Human evolution is the eternal revealing of the Self to the selves.' In the processes of prayer a bridge between the selves is built upon which the self may stand, and surveying both can better bring about the unity of the two, for it is always the function of the bridge to unite those entities which desire to be together and which find their finest meaning only when they are together.

So prayer may well be called that high functioning of the self that is seeking in its unity to find the fulfilment of the selves. In this unity the body may find its health, the mind its meaning and the spirit its peace.

15

New Possibilities for Achieving a Healthy Spirit

I have been trying to look at health in a broad context. I believe that all there is of man is bound together in a functioning unity. While the nature of man may reveal many complexities, they are centred in a unity of being that makes it inevitable that there is a constant interplay of the elements of being.

I have looked at the new insights of medicine that verify this working unity. I have explored in depth some of the old concepts of religion and philosophy to see what they say to the newer ideas about man's health. I believe there is some warrant for feeling that the old in experience and the new in research can be brought into a harmonious and fruitful relationship.

A new sense of the awareness of personal responsibility in the healing process appears to be emerging spontaneously in many directions. At luncheon in the Doctor's Club at the Texas Medical Center just last week a physician told me, 'I now share all my information with my patients. I lay out the charts and the findings of our testing and say to the patient, "This is what we have found out about you. Now there are several ways in which we can proceed in trying to manage your case and we would like your judgment at this point." ' And the physician added that in addition to removing almost completely the possibility of malpractice suits, this approach engages the patient more completely in the treatment process. This seems to add another useful dimension to healing as personal responsibility is added to medical skill.

What happens here, of course, is a recognition of the fact that the decision-making process may be important for the patient's welfare, for the nature of the decisions can be guided. The patient may decide that he does not like the doctor, or is uncomfortable about the choice of alternatives that has been made. Then he may unconsciously drag his heels and so slow up the healing process. Decision-making at one level or another is almost constant. But to guide and direct this process so that it becomes a part of the positive approach to healing appears to be a more recently discovered resource for the physician to employ.

While less tangible, the spiritual nature of man is no less real, especially in its impact on his health. The essential nature of faith works to marshal the resources of the being into positive action towards the goals of his own self-fulfilment. Too often people have invested their capacity for faith in something or someone. But at its best it is not so much a matter of faith in as it is faith 'that'. The faith that is invested in self-fulfilling action is apt to be more significant in affecting a person's response to life than that of projecting faith outward. I am sure that Maslow's studies have many times verified that people of low degrees of self-fulfilment and self-actualization thought they were people of faith. Their misfortune was that they used their capacity for faith partially or negatively. The self-actualizing person organizes his faith as an inner form of energy to make him confident in himself and his goals. Those who do not have this inner security may be 'blown about by every wind of doubt' until their capacity has been reduced to a meaningless echo-chamber.

Too often in the past organized religions have taken man's capacity for faith and have channelled it to the advantage of the institution. This has led to a personal retreat from responsibility. The adherent to the institution was supplied with a number of scapegoats who were made responsible for the things that happened in life. Recently I explored a number of the magnificent pyramids in Mexico. More than two thousand of these monuments were built to the numerous gods who were respon-

sible for every aspect of existence. There was a strenuous effort to make sure that every god was properly appeased. The gods were the cause of life's events, good or bad, and man's responsibility was to the gods rather than to himself.

More modern practices have refined and made more sophisticated the scapegoats of life, but they continue to exist and compromise man's responsibility to himself. Whether it be a God or a physician who is made into an all powerful scapegoat, the individual's responsibility for his own life is reduced, and to that degree the creative energy of faith is misdirected. Any form of religion or medical practice that presents an omnipotent image undermines the obligation for personal responsibility that each individual must assume.

True worthship

Many forms of worship have existed in the past. Many have practised human degradation or diminished appreciation of the self. True worship in the context I would employ would be committed to elevating the value of self and to the process of moving a person toward fuller self-realization.

Each person is engaged in a struggle to find the richest meaning for his or her own life. Some call this a theology. Some call it a philosophy. Perhaps we might refer to it as the point where a person achieves his or her highest appreciation for the inner kingdom of spirit.

This meaningful inner state is achieved when he finds a practical working relationship between his own concept of the universe, his cosmology, and his concept of himself, his psychology. This is the point where he finds his inner unity and his comfortable relationship with the beyond-self. When he achieves this state he discovers that the dividing line between self-repair and self-fulfilment evaporates.

Let's look at our cosmology. Man once felt himself to be a part of a universe which threatened his life and buffeted him without reason in little understood cosmic forces. As his view of the universe changed, so his idea of himself was modified. Now

in a day of nuclear physics and ultimate non-materiality, man can perceive of himself as a part of a realm of law and order with which he can conform and grow in self-mastery as well as cosmic inter-relationship. The self discovers its value within this cosmic order to the degree that it masters the disciplines that make it possible for the resources of being to be developed to their highest potential.

Our psychology is essentially our view of ourself and our behaviour in relation to our inner being and the world about us. Man once thought of himself as a creature unique in all creation because of God's special interest in him. Then he thought of himself as a highly refined animal with special endowments. More recently he has thought of himself as related to all of nature but possessed of a uniqueness of consciousness which was both a burden and a privilege. If he managed his consciousness wisely and well he could find a rich and fulfilling life, but if his consciousness became perverted he could misdirect the powers of being in such a way that his life could become a chamber of horrors.

At the point where his cosmology and psychology meet in the integrative processes of living, man creates his own sense of life's meaning. If he values his place in creation and the wonder of his uniqueness he may be able to discover the self-concept that can move him towards self-actualization and a state of super-health in body, mind and spirit.

He may deliberately engage in worth-creating activities, in religion, in the arts, or in meditation, that are designed to enhance his sense of self-worth. Or he may spontaneously engage in creative activities in groups or individually that make him feel good about himself and the life he lives.

The struggle to give worth to life is basic to true health. The more we value life, the more we will seek to bring it to full actualization. The more we are absorbed in creative expression of self, the less we will be apt to misdirect the energy of being into the internal conflicts that are acted out in illness. So part of our responsibility for our own health may be found in discovering new and valid means of worship or in rediscovering

revitalizing old ways that have had their value in the past but have been obscured by our preoccupation with a new cosmology and psychology.

Bringing life into focus

The implications for more vigorous health that may be found in the new interest of physical and personality scientists in man's nature are worth exploring. If life can be made significant enough to integrate all of the experience of life in a new perspective, all of life must feel the impact of this philosophical upswing.

In an age of technology men have focused on the objective realities. The science of the nineteenth century was preoccupied with the control of the external world. Men almost forgot that there was an inner kingdom. But science has rediscovered the subjective. The methods of twentieth-century science make the subjective as real as the objective, though obviously different not only in experience but in the methods by which it would be explored.

No less a physicist than Edwin Schrödinger has pointed out,

> The spirit is to an eminent degree subject and this evades objective examination. . . In this sense all science is a doctrine of the objective. . . The spirit can never strictly speaking be the object of scientific inquiry, because objective knowledge of the spirit is a contradiction of terms. Yet, on the other hand, all knowledge relates to the spirit, or more properly, exists in it, and this is the whole reason for our interest in any field of knowledge whatsoever.

The validity of man's spiritual experience is of a different order of reality from that of the method and mood of the laboratory researcher.

The mood and method of speculative physics does not ignore Newton's place in the history and development of modern science, but his concept of reality seems strangely irrelevant to the perception we now have of the universe. But were there no

such scientific judgment, the intuitive, essentially spiritual judgments of man concerning himself would remain unaffected. For man as the subject is the knowing creature, and he cannot be judged by what he knows or does not know as much as by what he is and is able to do with what he knows. The subjective way by which he experiences himself is more essential to his responsibility for his health and wholeness than all the terms he may know to designate a multitude of physical symptoms. This courage to affirm a great and sustaining faith in all of life is a subjective achievement which does not depend on science, even though it may be supported by it.

This affirmation will build on knowledge, but will include intuition, mystical revelation and a firm faith in the ultimate reality of the subjective response to all that is experienced. Here a variety of creative emotional responses will be employed, calling forth from the conscious and extra-conscious levels of being those responses that move toward a structural relationship between creature and Creator. Surely, if such a structural relationship and response is built into the lower forms of life, both organic and inorganic, it would seem inevitable that such a response would be innate with the most spiritually sensitive form of creation, man. So it is not so much a matter of verifying its possibility in man as it is of affirming it with such courage that the affirmation becomes the basis for seasoning all the rest of man's knowledge and practice.

The most significant part of life for healthful living appears to be this creative and courageous affirmation of the value of being in the face of many of the evidences of an assault on being and the threat of non-being. It is not a matter of whistling in the dark, or believing what you know is not so. Rather it is claiming the right to verify the life-affirming nature of the subjective which can lead to self-actualization and the super-healthy state of being. It is the process of using the skills of mental discipline to realize the energizing resources of the spiritual nature to bring all of life into right relationship with the self that lives beyond reductionism in a state of transcendent perception.

The treasure house within

If there is any one thing that has characterized the humanist exploration in psychology, it is the basic assumption that man may be far more wonderful in his creative endowment and spiritual nature than he has ever dared believe. Man cannot easily explain all there is of himself by reducing himself to constrictive scientific examination. Coulson, the atomic physicist, asserts,

> There is no hypothesis capable of explaining the birth of life, the development of consciousness, without the intervention of a factor that can be described as extra-scientific or supernatural.[1]

Deep within man is an integrative process at work that brings together in a living unity the major force-fields that influence man and his life. There appears to be at work in man something equivalent to the Pauli Principle at work in atoms. With the Pauli Principle all creation is held together by what might be spoken of as an innate courtesy among energy charges that works to give substance and structure to atoms. Within man a capacity for consciousness appears to be at work to integrate experience, insight, and revelation in a way that gives substance and structure to life.

When Freud looked into the depths of man's consciousness, he saw reservoirs of primitive drives and compelling appetites that could thwart the higher consciousness of man. Jung, more optimistic, saw in the consciousness the accumulated wisdom, racial experience and human potential that could aid man in his growth toward a more fulfilled and creative being. Maslow saw a capacity to learn ways of growing in creativity as well as the perception that could lead toward wise, fulfilled and super-healthy living.

Looking at the potential of man for internal development, Margenau expresses the physicist's view. 'It is my firm conclusion that there is room for a formal principle which will extend relativity and exclusion into the world of the living. Modern

physics is by no means hostile to such a notion, which has sometimes been described as a principle of resonance.' It does not seem unreasonable, then, to think that in man's highly organized consciousness he might develop and use a capacity for resonance that could make possible his higher spiritual perception. Then resonance and revelation could supplement each other in the innate and achieved manifestations of the higher consciousness. Then the inner kingdom would give meaning and purpose to the observations of science, and the treasure-house within would pour its riches into fulfilled living.

The treasure-house of being that enriches the self-concept and with it the inner health of the individual may be explored at three levels. First would be the process of therapeutic meditation. Second would be the perception of creative evolution that is moving man towards a great sense of worth. Third would be the transpersonal experience, the psychic overflow or the sense of meaning that comes with the mystical experience.

Meditation as a component of personal fulfilment is being explored by competent psychologists like Rogers, Ornstein and LeShan. The purpose is to understand what the disciplines of meditation can contribute towards the wise use of consciousness. Carefully designed exercises, not dissimilar from those used in monastic orders, are employed to move the self towards a perception of the deep self that motivates life at the same time that the skills of wise self-management are stimulated. This is the inverse of the method that is so often observed with the physically and emotionally disturbed, who allow their minds to fret and worry and in this process undermine the creative relationship that should exist between mind and spirit. The mind will be at work influencing life in any event. The undisciplined mind may create the conditions that lay life waste. The guided consciousness may act on experience with a wisdom that reduces its threat and restores a person to the wholeness that is bound up with creative purpose and fruitful will-power.

If a person feels that all his individual effort and man's long struggle are to no purpose, it can produce a deep despair. If man is convinced that all he does is useless, for nothing comes

of it but death and failure, he cannot easily avoid depression.
Pierre Teilhard de Chardin feels that all of life is committed to
a cosmic purpose that moves toward greater heights of spiritual
realization. In this he finds,

> A zest for living. . . which would appear to be the fundamental
> driving force which impels and directs the universe along its
> main axis of complexity-consciousness.[2]

A fundamentally psychic nature of evolution,

> may work intellectually and affectively to release and heigh-
> ten in ourselves, and provide a base for ever more powerful
> rational motives and inducements for living.[3]

This, then, gives to life a constant verification that is its own
best proof. Put simply, the self that believes greatly in the
purpose of life tends to act on that premise and in so doing fulfils
the meaning of purpose in personal terms. If the failure of
meaning leads to depression and illness, the achievement of
meaning points the way towards hope and the physical evidences of a hope fulfilled. Should this fail to be realized in
personal terms, the failure may be absorbed in a cosmic purpose
that is larger than the individual.

The perception that comes as the end-result of wise discipline
and significant meaning may show itself in that crowning
achievement of consciousness, the moment of mystical illumination. This experience of cosmic awareness, this moment of
transcendence, this opening of the perception, may evade the
seeker even while it challenges his quest. But for those who
know these moments of illumination, a new measure of wholeness floods the being. Those who experience it never can quite
find the words to describe it, but those who share the experience
know its undeniable validity. A wise and skilful physician who
had this dimension of consciousness burst in upon his life
unsought, said with a sense of awe, 'It was the most real thing
that has ever happened to me in my whole life'. The psychic
overflow takes all there is of life and gives to it a significance and
integrity that makes it all one in a fulfilling awareness of

transcendent meaning. When that occurs, there is no longer doubt, fear or a preoccupation with personal failure. Something deep within the self is discovered that is larger than self as it becomes at home or at one with all else that is.

These steps to meaning turn the depths of the self into a reservoir of beauty and a treasure house of wonder, awe and fulfilment.

Group life that inspires

Often the moments of illumination that provide the resources for the super-healthy orientation of life come in a shared time of group experience. I have just come from three days of sharing with twenty-five persons who are engaged in various forms of psychotherapy. Several times a year we meet together to consider the development and health of our spirits. Most of the members of the group would hesitate to designate themselves as religious in the usual construction of that word. But each member of the group has discovered a core of being that grows and profoundly influences life, attitudes toward the self and attitudes towards other persons and their needs.

In the period of several years that we have worked together to develop and enrich our inner beings there have been interesting and sometimes subtle changes taking place. With the authority that society grants its healers there is at times a sense of omnipotence that grows within the psychotherapist. As a person sustains his sense of worth by externally provided evidence he may come to be so dependent upon this that he neglects his own inner being. In the disciplines of group action there appears to be a withering away of this manufactured omnipotence as a deeper and richer form of self-verification grows. The group with common purpose and strenuous disciplines discovers ways to inner wholeness that are more authentic and less deceptive than those that superficially sustain the insecure person. The group process provides both the incentives and correctives for important growth.

In the disciplines of the group we develop skills in paying

attention to life, to others and to ourselves as we relate to others and their lives. We find a mysterious and wonderful process at work. A resonance to life emerges in the group. The more we pay attention to others, the more we discover within ourselves. And the more we discover in the depths of our own being, the more we perceive in the movement of the life-force in those about us who invite our attention. In this relationship of self to self and self to others, life changes. As Coulson, the physicist, puts it,

> Suppose that we are studying a piece of crystal or a flower. By studying them, and formulating laws about them, we cannot be said to alter them. They are effectively the same after we have finished studying them as they were before we began. But suppose instead that we try to study ourselves, and ask ourselves questions about ourselves. Then, immediately, we begin to affect and change ourselves.[4]

And in the vibrant and challenging life of a group the many-faceted encounters with spirit-endowed life may produce the most significant form of growth and change we can know.

It has been the experience of this group that we can create a spiritual family and discover a psychic home. We commonly find self-healing in our disciplined search. We can learn to direct the energy of life toward healthful living. We come together worn and threatened by the burdens of our role in life and soon find that we gain strength from each other. Our minds and spirits go through a healing process and almost invariably our bodies show the results of it. Arthritic pains disappear, sinuses clear up, functional disturbances are reduced and a general feeling of euphoria develops.

Many of the traditionally employed group processes may have developed through the years in response to this need to work out deep feelings. The theatre, sports and vacations may spontaneously serve to relieve stress. How much more fully these needs might be met if the group processes of life could be enriched with more significant and disciplined action. Greater

health might well be one of the fruits of skilfully directed sharing of the resources of mind, emotion and spirit.

Whole beings in a broken society

Perhaps more than we realize, the impinging of social stress upon life weakens our resistance to disease and wears down our resistance to illness.

Many of the disillusioning revelations of our day with their destructive implications for group life may produce suspicion, depression and anxiety.

When social crises are acute, it is more than ever necessary for people to look within for the resources that can help them to manage crises and maintain wholeness of being.

People become ill because of their internal and external environment. Each person needs to realize that he is a part of his own environment. He needs to shield himself from the destructive influences both within and without by a determined effort to grow more competent in accepting responsibility for his thoughts, his emotions and his health.

During this exploration of our personal responsibility for our own health I trust I have not only shown some of the facts about psychosomatic illness and the research that is related to it. I hope that I have also looked with fresh interest at the endowment we possess as persons who can preside over their own thought processes. When we can learn important skills in self-management and meditation, we can also begin to discover that true wholeness is not merely a matter of seeing a doctor but rather of seeing to ourselves.

Then people who learn to manage their own attitudes towards personal responsibility and disciplined action can contribute significantly to their own well-being. They will not then find themselves as fractured images of a fracturing and troubled society. Rather, they may find that the need for strength creates strength, as the need for a more healthful society calls forth the best efforts of the individual who would make himself whole. Anyone can resonate to a problem and add to it. It is a finer

order of human effort to create the skills that overcome problems through developing the super-healthy person who can make his contribution to man's next step in evolutionary growth.

BIBLIOGRAPHY

Alexander, Franz G., *Psychosomatic Medicine*, Norton, New York 1950

American Foundation, *Medical Research*, Little Brown, Boston 1955

Andrews, D. H., *The Symphony of Life*, Unity Books, New York 1966

Bakan, David, *Disease, Pain and Sacrifice*, University of Chicago Press 1968

Barlow, D. H., *Behavioral Assessment of Adult Disorders*, Guildford, New York 1981

Beard, Rebecca, *Everyman's Search*, Merrybrook Press, Wells, Vermont 1950

Brena, S. F., *Yoga and Medicine*, Penguin Books 1972

Carrel, Alexis, *Man, the Unknown*, Harper, New York 1935

Coulson, C. A., *Science and Christian Belief*, Oxford University Press 1955

Dampier, W. C., and Whetham, M. D., *A History of Science*, Macmillan, New York 1931

Davis, Charles, *Body as Spirit*, Seabury Press, New York 1976

Dubos, René, *Mirage of Health*, Doubleday Anchor, New York 1961

Duke, Marc, *Acupuncture*, Pyramid House, New York 1972

Dunbar, Flanders, *Emotions and Bodily Changes*, Columbia University Press 1954

—, *Your Child's Mind and Body*, Random House, New York 1949

Edman, Irwin, *The Philosophy of Santayana*, Scribners, New York 1953

Einstein, Albert, *Cosmic Religion*, Covici Friede, New York 1931

Frank, Jerome, *Persuasion and Healing*, Johns Hopkins Press, Baltimore 1961

Frankl, Victor, *The Doctor and the Soul*, Alfred Knopf, New York 1955

Grinker, Roy R., *Psychosomatic Research*, Evergreen, New York 1961

Halliday, J. H., *Psychosocial Medicine*, Norton, New York 1948

Hardy, Alister, *The Spiritual Nature of Man*, Oxford University Press 1979

Hastings, A. C., *Health for the Whole Person*, Westview Books, Boulder, Colorado 1980

Hora, Thomas, *Dialogues in Metapsychiatry*, Seabury Press, New York 1977

James, William, *The Will to Believe*, Longmans Green 1902

Jonas, Gerald, *Visceral Learning*, Viking Books, New York 1973

Karagulla, Shafica, *Breakthrough to Creativity*, DeVorss, Los Angeles 1968

Koestler, Arthur, *Beyond Reductionism*, Beacon Books, Boston 1968

Laing, R. D., *The Self and Others*, Penguin Books 1972

LeShan, Lawrence, *You Can Fight for Your Life*, Evans, New York 1977

Lynch, James J., *The Broken Heart*, Basic Books, New York 1977

Madow, Leo, *Anger*, Scribners, New York 1972

Martin, Barclay, *Anxiety and Neurotic Disorders*, Wiley 1971

McNeill, J. T., *A History of the Cure of Souls*, Harper 1951

Meerloo, Joost A., *The Rape of the Mind*, World Publications, New York 1956

Meister, David, *Hypochondria*, Taplinger, New York 1980

Melzack, Ronald, *The Puzzle of Pain*, Basic Books, New York 1973

Ornstein, Robert E., *The Psychology of Consciousness*, Viking Books 1972

Pellegrino, Edmund, *Medicine and Philosophy*, Yale University Press 1974

Rhine, J. B., *PSI*, Harper and Row 1975

Russell, Bertrand, *The Impact of Science on Society*, Allen and Unwin 1953

Sobel, David S. (ed.), *Ways of Health: Holistic Approaches to Ancient and Contemporary Medicine*, Harcourt Brace 1979

Tournier, Paul, *Guilt and Grace*, Hodder & Stoughton 1962

Ullmann, Montague, *Dream Telepathy*, Macmillan, New York 1973

Underhill, Evelyn, *Mysticism*, Methuen 1949

Wallnofer, Heinrich, *Chinese Folk Medicine*, Signet Books 1972

Weatherhead, L. S., *Psychology and Life*, Hodder & Stoughton 1934

—, *Psychology, Religion and Healing*, Hodder & Stoughton 1951

Weiss, E., and English, Spurgeon, *Psychosomatic Medicine*, W. B. Saunders 1943

NOTES

Chapter 1

1. Aldous Huxley, *The Observer*, London 22 October 1961, quoted by Marc Duke, *Acupuncture*, Pyramid House, New York 1972, p. 9.

2. Duke, op. cit., p. 92.

3. Duke, op. cit., p. 15.

4. Gerald Jonas, *Visceral Learning*, Viking Books, New York 1973. The quotation comes from the front flap of the dust jacket.

5. Leonard Cottrell, *Identity and Interpersonal Competence*, University of Chicago Press 1955, pp. 434f.

6. S. F. Brena, *Yoga and Medicine*, Penguin Books 1972, p. xiv.

7. Brena, op. cit., pp. 21–4.

8. Brena, op. cit., p. 126.

9. Edward Podolsky MD, in a reprint from the *Philadelphia Enquirer*, 21 January 1940.

10. Edward A. Strecker and Kenneth E. Appel, in *Journal of the American Psychiatric Association*, May 1942.

11. E. Weiss and Spurgeon English, *Psychosomatic Medicine*, W. B. Saunders 1943, p. 3.

12. Leo Madow, *Anger*, Scribners, New York 1972, Cf. p. 71: 'The task of the physician is to enable man through understanding of the laws governing his energy economy to use energy for healthy living. Energy misused creates susceptibility to disease and endangers life.'

13. This quotation comes from material preserved in my class notebook.

Chapter 2

1. For this material see Jerome Frank, *Persuasion and Healing*, Johns Hopkins Press, Baltimore 1961.

2. Jerome Frank, *American Journal of Psychiatry* Vol. 79, pp. 345–51.

3. Jerome Frank, *American Journal of Psychiatry* Vol. 115, pp. 961–8.

4. Jerome Frank, *Archives of Neurology and Psychiatry* Vol. 77, pp. 283–99.

Chapter 3

1. Victor Frankl, *The Doctor and the Soul*, Alfred Knopf, New York 1955, p. 83.

2. Frankl, op. cit., p. 267.

3. Max Planck, *Scientific Autobiography*, Greenwood Press, Westport, Ct 1968. The quotation comes from the last page of the book.

4. Romain Rolland, *Mahatma Gandhi*, The Century Publishing Co 1924, p. 56.

5. This material derives from transcripts of the Wainwright House Seminar entitled *Fifth Spiritual Healing Seminar*, Wainwright House Publications, Rye, New York 1956.

6. Flanders Dunbar, *Emotions and Bodily Changes*, Columbia University Press, New York 1954, p. 63; cf. p. 40: 'It is impossible to regard activity as a sum of reflexes unless you put a psychic idea into your reflexes. Thus Schidler insists on the reality of the psychic factor in the whole picture.'

7. E. Weaver Johnson (Rebecca Beard), in *Everyman's Search*, Merrybrook Press, Wells, Vermont 1950; cf. p. 38: 'The cause is within us. The cure is within us. When we know this, our concept of disease is no longer that of something fixed upon the body cells which must be purged, cut or burned away. It is not something coming in from the outside which we cannot prevent. Rather it is a change from within, and we must find the reason why the body changes its perfect pattern to vibrate to discord rather than to harmony. Psychosomatic research is helping us find the clues. Incidentally, it is changing the whole attitude of medicine towards the problem of sick bodies and confused minds.'

8. Franz G. Alexander, *Psychosomatic Medicine. Its Principles and Applications*, Norton, New York 1950, pp. 133ff. Cf. Dunbar, op. cit., p. 226: 'Tension, repressed hostility and resentment have been recognized as factors in the aetiology of arthritis. It has been suggested that emotional disturbances, producing changes in the neuro-endocrine system, may cause derangements in the metabolism of the joint and may thus be instrumental in producing the clinical picture of arthritis.'

9. Dunbar, op. cit., p. 373: 'Studies of reaction to persistent low grade, everyday stresses and strains involving anger, guilt, rage,

frustration and so on, indicated that many symptoms of cardiovascular disorder were attributable to alterations of function which represented reactions to life stress.'

10. Quoted from the Wainwright House Seminar reports (see n. 5 above).

Chapter 4

1. Cecil G. Shaps, in *New Frontiers of Aging*, ed. Wilmar Donohue and Clark Tibbetts, University of Michigan Press, Ann Arbor, Michigan 1957, ch. 14.

2. There is a more recent study by Lawrence LeShan, *You Can Fight for Your Life*, Evans, New York 1977: 'There may be a good reason why clinical science has not solved the riddle of cancer. The answer may not lie within the realm of science at all. It may in fact be in the mind and emotions. After two decades of research and psychotherapeutic work with cancer patients Lawrence LeShan offers new evidence and some startling insights into why some individuals get cancer and others do not – and why some cancer patients are able to fight successfully for their lives while others rapidly succumb to the disease.'

3. In *The Cancer Dialogue*, October 1980, a conference of top authorities of the world exploring cancer research and the current state of knowledge about cancer, Dr Norman Shealy, a neurosurgeon and head of a treatment centre in Wisconsin, affirmed that prayer may yet be discovered to be the most effective resource for fighting cancer through recreating the inner climate that activates the body's own immunological resources to resist the development of neoplasts. (Statement recorded on tapes in my possession.)

Chapter 5

1. Dr Lawrence E. Hinkle and Dr Harold G. Wolff, from the Study Program in Human Health and Ecology of Man at New York Hospital and Cornell Medical Center, read at the 105th annual meeting of the American Medical Association; in *The Creative Power of the Mind*, Prentice-Hall 1957, p. 203.

2. Louis S. Reed, *The Healing Cults*, University of Chicago Press 1932, quoted by Jerome Frank, *Persuasion and Healing*, p. 103.

3. Gerald Heard, *Natural Theology*, p. xvii.

Chapter 6

1. Quoted by Shafica Karagulla, *Breakthrough to Creativity*, DeVorss and Co., Los Angeles 1968, p. 224.

Chapter 7

1. J. A. Hadfield, in *The Spirit*, ed. B. H. Streeter, Macmillan 1919, pp. 103f.

Chapter 8

1. George Santayana, *Scepticism and Animal Faith*, Constable 1923.

Chapter 9

1. William James, *The Will to Believe*, Longmans Green 1902. Cf. id., *Varieties of Religious Experience*, Longmans Green 1903, p. 208: 'There are only two ways in which it is possible to get rid of anger, fear, despair, or other undesirable affections. One is that an opposite affection would break over us, and the other is by getting so exhausted with the struggle that we have to stop – so we drop down, give up and don't care any longer.'

Chapter 10

1. Alexis Carrel, *Man the Unknown*, Harper 1935, pp. 198f.
2. Carrel, op. cit., pp. 124f.
3. Albert Einstein, *Cosmic Religion*, Covici Friede, New York 1931, pp. 49f., 53f.

Chapter 13

1. Bernard Holland, introduction to Jakob Boehme, *Three Dialogues of the Supersensual Life*.
2. Quoted by Evelyn Underhill, *Mysticism*, Methuen 1949.
3. A. Clutton Brock, in *The Spirit*, ed. B. H. Streeter, Macmillan 1919, pp. 304–9.
4. Raynor Carey Johnson, *The Imprisoned Splendor*, Harper and Bros, New York 1953.
5. George Russell Harrison, *What Man May Be*, William Morrow and Co, New York 1956.

Chapter 14

1. Alexis Carrel, *Man the Unknown*, Harper 1935, pp. 146f.
2. Carrel, op. cit., pp. 147f.
3. Carrel, op. cit., pp. 144f.

Chapter 15

1. C. A. Coulson, *Science and Christian Belief*, Oxford University Press 1955.

2. Teilhard de Chardin, *The Phenomenon of Man*, Collins and Harper and Row 1965, p. 24.

3. Teilhard de Chardin, *The Activation of Energy*, Collins and Harcourt Brace, New York 1970, p. 23.

4. Coulson, op. cit., p. 94.

The Role of Faith in the
Process of Healing